Weaving on (

Marianne Barnes

Schiffer Publishing Ltd

4880 Lower Valley Road Atglen, Pennsylvania 19310

FOR SUPPLIES CONTACT:
THE COUNTRY SEAT, INC.
1013 OLD PHILLY PIKE
KEMPTON, PA 19529
610-756-6124

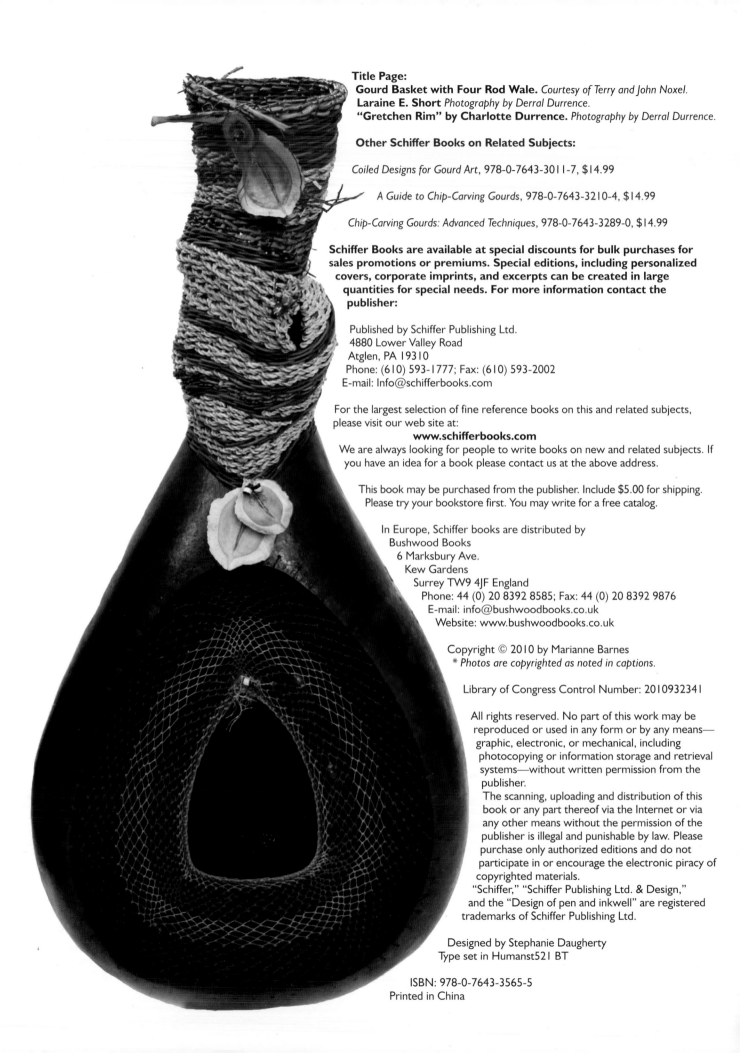

Title Page:
Gourd Basket with Four Rod Wale. *Courtesy of Terry and John Noxel.*
Laraine E. Short *Photography by Derral Durrence.*
"Gretchen Rim" by Charlotte Durrence. *Photography by Derral Durrence.*

Other Schiffer Books on Related Subjects:

Coiled Designs for Gourd Art, 978-0-7643-3011-7, $14.99

A Guide to Chip-Carving Gourds, 978-0-7643-3210-4, $14.99

Chip-Carving Gourds: Advanced Techniques, 978-0-7643-3289-0, $14.99

Schiffer Books are available at special discounts for bulk purchases for sales promotions or premiums. Special editions, including personalized covers, corporate imprints, and excerpts can be created in large quantities for special needs. For more information contact the publisher:

Published by Schiffer Publishing Ltd.
4880 Lower Valley Road
Atglen, PA 19310
Phone: (610) 593-1777; Fax: (610) 593-2002
E-mail: Info@schifferbooks.com

For the largest selection of fine reference books on this and related subjects, please visit our web site at:
www.schifferbooks.com
We are always looking for people to write books on new and related subjects. If you have an idea for a book please contact us at the above address.

This book may be purchased from the publisher. Include $5.00 for shipping. Please try your bookstore first. You may write for a free catalog.

In Europe, Schiffer books are distributed by
Bushwood Books
6 Marksbury Ave.
Kew Gardens
Surrey TW9 4JF England
Phone: 44 (0) 20 8392 8585; Fax: 44 (0) 20 8392 9876
E-mail: info@bushwoodbooks.co.uk
Website: www.bushwoodbooks.co.uk

Designed by Stephanie Daugherty
Type set in Humanst521 BT

ISBN: 978-0-7643-3565-5
Printed in China

Contents

Dedication

To my wonderful husband, Jim. He is my main supporter, critic, and cheerleader. He also cuts and cleans all my gourds. A gourd artist couldn't have it any better!

Acknowledgments

Many thanks go to my wonderful gourd friends, especially the Gourdettes: Becky Folsom, Charlotte Durrence, Judy Poulson, Laraine Short, Peggy Hoffmaster, and Peggy Ash. We have spent many fun filled weeks in the mountains and in Florida playing with gourds and learning from each other, and another special thanks to Becky for volunteering to proofread my book.

I must mention the Upper South Carolina BasketMakers' Guild, as that is where I got my start in weaving, and a thank you goes to Sandy Roback who originally formed the group. Thanks, Sandy!

Thanks also to the faithful members of the Palmetto Gourd Patch and the South Carolina Gourd Society who have encouraged and supported me and I cannot forget my friends on the Gourd Patch website and my Facebook™ friends who were so excited about this book that many e-mailed me to preorder.

After submitting many pictures for some of Jim Widess' books, he suggested that I should write my own. Thanks, Jim, for that encouragement. My photographers, Kelly and Dorothy, were wonderful and so talented and very patient with me.

Last of all, thanks goes to Betsey Sloan, who inspired me as she took the first step to write her own book, *InLace Resin Technique*, and to Jennifer, my current editor who put it all together, and Tina, my first editor, who encouraged me and said, "Slow and steady wins the race. Keep plugging along!"

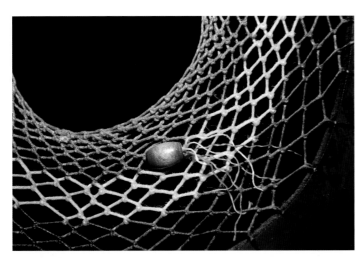

You might say that texture is the key element in my gourd weaving. Texture is playful and moves the eye up, down and around the gourd. It excites the eye with color and movement, yet the spokes coming from the top of the gourd gives a clean natural line of sophistication. When I think of a gourd, I think of something natural that comes from a seed placed in the ground. That is why weaving with natural elements like knobby yarns and mohair, sea grass, and cedar bark enrich the gourd. All the natural elements flow together and create a landscape of color and texture.

I wrote this book in order to help you learn how to weave baskets on top of a gourd. You will hear about how I was inspired to transfer my basket weaving to a gourd and the basket makers who inspired me. You will also learn safety procedures, the tools and equipment you will need, how to prepare the gourd, and how to choose the materials for weaving. You will also learn basket-weaving techniques that work well on top of a gourd. Twine, triple twine (also called three rod wale), twill, and undulating tapestry weaving will create interesting designs that incorporate the natural materials you will be using in the weaving process. You will learn several techniques for ending the basket weaving. This is called the rim.

After learning these techniques, you can create many different gourd baskets just by varying the different techniques, materials, and colors. You can also change the look of the gourd by adding extra elements to the gourd itself. Additionally, you can incorporate carving, painting, or pyrography techniques in creating the finished gourd. One element I like to add to my gourd basket is a dreamcatcher. It is added to the front of the gourd and resembles a spider web. You will learn several variations of how to make a dreamcatcher to add to your gourd weaving. Dreamcatchers are an authentic Native American tradition, believed to originate from the Ojibway tribe. I have a friend and fellow gourd artist of Cherokee heritage who told me what she knew about dream catchers. She said that according to the tradition practiced by that tribe, Ojibway dreamcatchers were made of sinew and willow. They are hung over a child's bed and catch the bad dreams allowing the good dreams to go through. She said she still had one in her room and her children

Dreamcatcher. *Photography by Kelly Hazel.*

Undulating Tapestry Gourd. *Photography by Dorothy Kozlowski.*

also had dreamcatchers over their beds. The Ojibway name for dreamcatcher means spider. Many other Native American tribes have added dreamcatchers to their traditions. While researching the dreamcatcher, I became interested in my own Native American heritage. Since there is Cherokee linage in my father's ancestry, I have been researching my Cherokee heritage.

Finally, you will learn how to add pizzazz to your gourd using beads, feathers, and other natural materials. You will also see some examples of gourd weaving and meet the artists who made them. Try the techniques and have fun coming up with your own style of weaving on gourds.

Finding Inspiration

When I moved to Greenville at the age of forty, I was starting a new life. Recently divorced, I wanted to do something different with my art. I had always been a watercolor painter and now wanted to take a new direction. I found a little shop downtown that offered basket-weaving classes. I took a few classes and then bought some books and patterns and taught myself many of the techniques. I met Sandy Elbrecht (she later married and became Sandy Elbrecht Roback), another art teacher, and she invited me to a meeting about starting a basket guild in Greenville. It is called the Upper South Carolina BasketMakers' Guild and it still meets monthly. So I became a charter member and started my journey with weaving. One month a member brought a gourd to the meeting and taught us how to cut it open and apply shoe polish to color it. I was "hooked." I started visualizing all the ways I could incorporate my weaving with the gourd.

"By the Sea." *Photography by Kelly Hazel.*

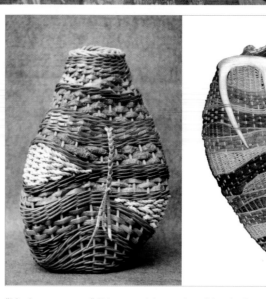

"Undercurrents." Woven with reed and barks in undulating rows. *Courtesy of Cass Schorsch. Scanned by Kelly Hazel.*

"Crosscurrents." This antler wall hanging shows an example of increasing and decreasing. *Courtesy of Cass Schorsch. Scanned by Kelly Hazel.*

Cass Schorsch

There are four basket weavers who really inspired me with the weaving techniques they use in their baskets. One was Cass Schorsch, a basket weaver from Michigan. Cass uses many natural materials to create texture in her baskets, and she was instrumental in the development of my basket weaving techniques on gourds. Cass became a great friend and was my source of cedar bark. I took a class from her at a state convention in North Carolina. The basket was called "Undercurrents." Cass used cedar and pine barks, seagrass, and reed and made it move or undulate throughout the basket. You can see these materials and techniques in her baskets.

The other picture is "Crosscurrents" and is woven with red pine, white pine, spruce, cedar bark, dyed rattan, and sea grass. I started thinking about how I could apply that technique to my gourds. I wanted to create a landscape with the materials I used and make it move. I wrote a pattern and gave Cass credit for the inspiration. I applied the techniques I learned from Cass, added my own materials and my own application of the techniques, and my "Undulating Gourd" was born. I used softer materials, such as yarns and mohair, to fill spaces, as well as the hard materials such as cedar bark, seagrass, and reed. By decreasing and increasing in the different areas of the weaving, the movement was achieved. This pattern is included in the book so be sure to try your hand at this gourd basket.

Sandy Elbrecht Roback

The second basket weaver who inspired me was Sandy Roback. She is a very good friend and was instrumental in getting me involved in basket weaving. Only one person could talk me into making a twill basket, and that was Sandy! I am not a master, but at least I use some twills in my weaving now. I admire the intricate designs created by twills. Since I have been researching my Cherokee ancestry, I have also

Twill Woven Basket by Sandy Roback. *Photography by Dorothy Kozlowski.*

researched some of the Cherokee baskets made with river cane that use the twill technique.

Sandy is a very precise basket weaver, and her specialty is weaving twill baskets. With her mathematical and analytical mind she creates her own designs. Her craftsmanship is awesome and the colors she uses in her baskets make them stand out. She is truly a professional. In the chapter on techniques, you will find Sandy's directions for designing and calculating a continuous twill pattern. Twills are beautiful and really make a wonderful gourd basket. You can use Sandy's twill technique instructions on a gourd. Just remember that you only have to do the sides, as the gourd is your base.

Jill Choate

A well-known antler basket maker and teacher, Jill's baskets have always inspired and fascinated me. Her baskets combine two wonderful weaving techniques, twining and rib construction. She also uses color in her triple twining to create spirals, zigzags, darts, and many other designs. I was just recently able to take a class from Jill. She was invited by my basket guild to come and teach workshops on antler basketry. I quickly signed up for a class. It was so much fun and I learned so much. Jill is down to earth and such a wonderful teacher. We became friends and she agreed to be a part of this book. I applied the techniques I learned from Jill to my gourd baskets and was excited at the results.

"Tripod" is woven with round reed using three rod wale and rib basketry. *Courtesy of Jill Choate.*

Flo Hoppe

I have to mention one other basket maker who influenced my work and that is Flo Hoppe. She wrote the book, *Wicker Basketry*, and the information in the book has helped me learn many new and different techniques using round reed. I met Flo in 1992 when I attended my first North Carolina Basket Convention. I won her basket in a raffle, and immediately went to one of the vendors and bought her book. I asked her to sign it and she very graciously wrote in the book, "To Marianne — Enjoy this book and the basket that you won. Happy Weaving! Flo Hoppe NCBA 1992." I have treasured the basket and book since and use the book as a source of very valuable information. The illustrations and directions are very easy to follow and is the best source of directions on weaving techniques using round reed that I have been able to find. She has also written a second book titled *Contemporary Wicker Basketry*. Flo has woven on gourds as well, so you will see some of these gourd baskets in my gallery of pictures.

"Carnival" is a round reed basket with spiraling and reverse spiraling and uses color for design. *Courtesy of Flo Hoppe.*

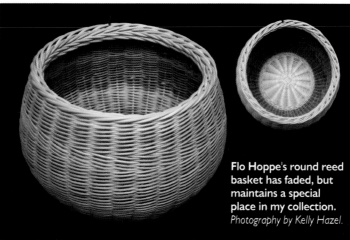

Flo Hoppe's round reed basket has faded, but maintains a special place in my collection. *Photography by Kelly Hazel.*

Chapter One

Gourd Safety

When it comes to working with gourds, you really need to be aware of the safety issues involving gourds, thus, this entire chapter dealing with this serious matter. It is so important that you protect yourself from any possible health issues. Gourds are wonderful and so much fun, and I do not want to scare any of you away from working with them. If you take the safety precautions and protect yourself, you will enjoy working with gourds so much that it will be worth the effort.

I have various safety tools depending on the task at hand. It is best to do the cleaning outside. Bringing moldy gourds into your home is dangerous. Mold spores can spread through your house. I always use gloves when handling gourds, especially if they are moldy and dirty. I also use a mask or respirator that I wear when working with gourds. I have a dust collector as well, so that when I work in the studio I can collect the dust from the gourds. I have a door to the studio that separates it from my living quarters. You never want to have gourds, especially cut gourds that have not been sealed, in your living quarters. If I use the gloves and masks, I never have a problem. Even when I am outside I use a mask and gloves.

Joy Jackson and Jerry Lewis organize a wonderful gourd event the first weekend in June every year at Cherokee, North Carolina, called the Gourd Artist Gathering. It is a weekend of raw gourd vendors, gourd art, gourd demonstrations, classes, and much more. Joy and Jerry wrote an article about gourd safety that really covers the basics you need to know. The Gourd Reserve (www.thegourdreserve.com) has much information on gourds, including Joy and Jerry's article on gourd safety. The Pennsylvania Gourd Society took the article and adapted it with Joy and Jerry's permission. I have permission to reprint it here. I hope this will inform you and help you stay safe while working with gourds.

Basics of Healthy Gourding

Are you allergic? If you are new to gourds, you will soon learn your sensitivities to them, if any, and the measures you'll need to take when working with them. A metallic taste in the mouth is often the first sign and coughing or sneezing with runny eyes and nose.

When I work on moldy gourds or carve, I try to work outside. I wear a mask, glasses, and an apron. *Photography by Kelly Hazel.*

When working with gourds, the following common sense measures and easy-to-find products will help keep you healthy and happily crafting. The measures and protective items mentioned below are the first steps to maintaining good health while working with gourds. They should be followed even if you don't notice any sensitivity at all.

- **Latex Gloves:** Avoid direct skin contact with moldy gourds that have not yet been cleaned. When scrubbing gourds, dishwashing gloves are recommended.

- **Leather Gloves:** Wear leather gloves when carving; they will protect you from cuts.

- **Mask or Respirator:** Airborne dust particles and mold spores from gourds should be avoided just as any other type of airborne particulate should be. A mask or respirator designed to prevent inhalation of these minute particles should be worn when cleaning the outside surface, sanding, cutting, and cleaning inside surfaces of a gourd.

- **Work Outside:** Work with gourds outside whenever possible. If you must work inside, make sure you have good ventilation and a dust control system is strongly recommended. Store dirty gourds outside or in a shed/garage, but never in the house.

- **Avoid Dust/Clean-up After:** Dust particles and mold spores will cling to clothing and hair. Keeping your hair covered while stirring up gourd dust or mold is a good preventive measure. Change into clean clothes and wash the ones you were wearing after working with gourds at any stage (cleaning, sanding, cutting, carving, etc.).

- **Glasses or Goggles:** Helps prevent dust particles from getting into your eyes when sanding or cutting a gourd.

- **Clothing:** Avoid loose garments because they can be dangerous when using power tools. Wear an apron to help protect your clothing from dirt and to keep getting caught by power tools.

- **Gripping Material:** Use of a waffle-like shelf liner in your lap will help keep the gourd from slipping out of your grip when you are working on it. You can sew the gripping fabric to the front of your apron so it is always available.

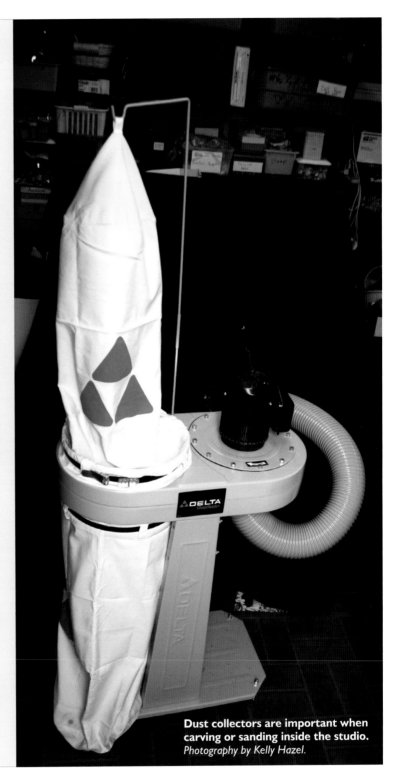

Dust collectors are important when carving or sanding inside the studio.
Photography by Kelly Hazel.

Information from My Online Friends

I have wonderful friends online. The online Yahoo™ group is called the Gourd Patch. If I have any questions about anything concerning gourds, I can email them and within a few minutes I have answers. They are so sharing with their information and offer the following tips about safety.

- **From Chris Pawlik**: "The pair of safety glasses I purchased from my eye doctor has a 1x magnification in them so I can see what I am working on. I have long hair so I keep it tied back and shower cap or surgical cap would work to keep the dust out of your hair. Use carvers tape (sports tape) on fingers and thumb when carving or weaving with waxed thread to keep if from cutting into your fingers."

- **From Susan Byra**: "Get some of those rubbery shelf liners. They help hold the gourd in one place on the table, your lap, etc. If you happen to be at Wal-Mart® when they are unpacking lamps, you can get some of the indented rounded Styrofoam® bottom pieces which will help hold larger gourds in one spot."

- **From Doris Trombley**: "If you keep your gourds wet inside and out while cleaning, you cut down on the mold floating around and you inhaling it."

- **From Dianne Schuler**: "When I weave, I make sure my work surface is steady, and there is enough space on the work surface for my supplies. I make sure there is plenty of good lighting. I have a small stool to prop my feet on and I get up about every hour or so to walk a bit."

- **From Darlene Propp**: "Safety is so important. Besides the obvious masks and respirators, which are vital to prevent lung conditions, and eye protectors when you are carving, one thing that is seldom mentioned is for long-haired people to tie their hair back or secure it somehow. I have gotten my hair caught in my drill and also burned it with my wood burner. Learned my lesson. Now it's short, but if it were still long I would be very careful with it."

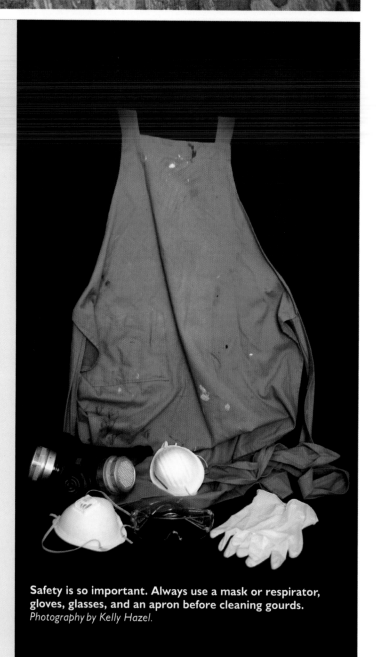

Safety is so important. Always use a mask or respirator, gloves, glasses, and an apron before cleaning gourds. *Photography by Kelly Hazel.*

Chapter Two

Preparing the Gourd

This chapter will help you get everything together and prepare everything before you start weaving. It seems that the bulk of the work involved in gourd weaving is preparing the gourd and gathering the materials. When all of this is done you can really have fun with the weaving. We will discuss the tools and equipment you will need, cleaning and cutting the gourd, drilling the holes needed, and applying any designs or color to the gourd that you want.

Tools and Equipment

I love my tools. They are necessary for what I want to do with the gourds. I think the most important ones are to protect you from the mold and dust from the gourd as you clean and cut it. Safety is so very important. You can seriously damage your lungs if you are not careful or get the "gourd flu" as some gourd artist calls it. Just follow safety measures talked about in the last chapter and you will have so much fun!

I have heard it said that a craftsman and an artist are only as good as their tools and equipment. Well, I don't know if that is true, but the correct tools sure make it easier. My husband loves to buy Christmas presents for me now. When he doesn't know what to get, he just buys a new gourd tool.

There are two basic kinds of tools: hand and power tools. You will need both. Some examples of the hand tools include sandpaper, scrubbers, large spoons, scrapers, cleanser, bucket

This extra large and thick kettle gourd is from California. The beautiful markings can be used by a gourd artist to create designs. *Photography by Kelly Hazel.*

Cleaning tools are important in preparing the gourd. *Photography by Kelly Hazel.*

Drills, saws, wood burner, and sander are tools used by the gourd artist. *Photography by Kelly Hazel.*

There are many good choices of gourds that can be prepared for weaving. *Photograph by Kelly Hazel.*

for water, and a pencil. For power tools you will need saws, drills, wood burner, and a sander. We will discuss the tools in more detail in the next sections. There are many suppliers for these wonderful tools. Check out the back of the book for a list of suppliers where I have found what I needed.

Selecting and Preparing Your Gourd

There are three main types of gourds: the ornamentals, the hard-shell, and the luffa. The ornamentals are the colorful ones you use in fall decorations and see at the grocery store. The inside of the luffa is like a sponge. Many people use them in the bath and shower to exfoliate their skin. The hard-shell gourds are the gourds used in this book. There are many different kinds of hard-shell gourds. I use gourds that, when the top is cut off, there is a bowl shape left for weaving. The ones I use most often are bottle gourds, kettle gourds, pear gourds, teardrop gourds, and martin gourds. Other gourds that can be used are canteen, apple, cannonball, bushel basket, and zucca gourds. To find out more information about gourds and growing them, read the book by Ginger Summit titled, *Gourds in Your Garden*. I really like to find thick gourds for my weaving. I prefer to place the spokes "on top" of the gourd's cut surface so that when I weave I have a nice clean line from the gourd to the top of the basket. Thick gourds can often be found from gourd suppliers from Arizona and California. Both states have a longer growing time, allowing the gourds to grow thick.

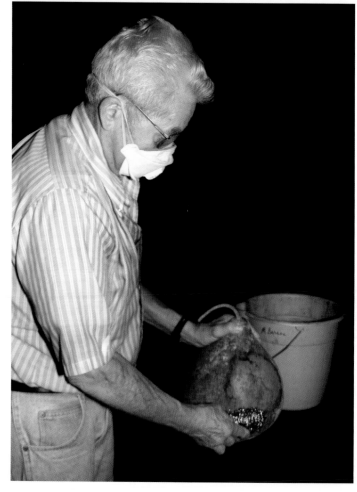

My husband Jim cleans the gourds outside, using a bucket of water and a scrubby. *Photography by Kelly Hazel.*

Cleaning the Outside

As I said in my dedication of the book, my husband cleans and cuts my gourds most of the time. He has become very good at doing this part of preparing the gourd. He usually fills up a tub with warm water and cleans the gourds outside on our deck. He uses a metal scrubby that he gets at the store. He says the stainless steel ones work best, but he also uses the copper ones. If the gourd is very hard to clean, he will wet it and pour an abrasive cleaner on it. This softens the grime and mold on the outside making it easier to clean.

Some gourd farms such as Ghost Creek Gourds in Laurens, South Carolina, provide already-cleaned gourds for purchase. Dickie and Linda Martin own the farm and have a gourd washing machine. It is a large steel tank about fifteen to twenty feet across with a circulating series of sprinklers above it. The continuous pressure of the water and the gourds moving around cleans them. It is always nice to be able to buy clean gourds. You can find Ghost Creek Gourds in the suppliers list.

Once again I went to my gourd friends. This time I asked my friends on Facebook™ about how they clean the outside of their gourds.

- **From Darlene Propp (who has been working with gourds since 1998):** "For the outside, I like to soak them in a tub and scrub them with a copper scrubby. Sometimes I line an old trash can with a black trash bag, then fill with water, put in the gourds and weigh them down with a brick or two on the lid, and let them soak for a day or so. And sometimes I just put them in the sink and go for it. I've also done some rot cleaning, and that works really well, especially if you want a clear surface for burning. It looks as nice as a green cleaned gourd, but you don't have to work so hard on it. Rot cleaning is when you cut an opening when they're green but mature, and put them in a vat of water (something with a lid). Leave them there for 2-3 weeks. You can change the water every now and then if you like. It will stink to high heaven, but the gourd comes out nice and clear with no mold markings. It is great for wood burning. And the gourd cures just that fast, too. No waiting a year. And because it's full of water, it doesn't implode or shrink. I accidentally cut a little gourd off the vine while it was still growing and tried it. Worked great. I want to try the boiling in peroxide, but haven't done it yet."

- **From Jane Huisingh:** "I use a pampered chef stone scraper to help scrape the outside."

- **From Judy Richie (who uses gourds from Arizona and California):** "Just put them in a tub and cover with damp potting soil and leave them a few days. The enzymes in the dirt eat away the skin. Then, just take them out and scrub a little to remove any remaining skin. I clean all my gourds like this. And, this includes the white baked on kind from Arizona and other hot climates. The big ones, I just put on the grass after they have been in the potting soil a few days and squirt them with the water hose. Most of the skin is gone and I only have to scrub a few places.

A scrubby can be used to remove the mold from the surface of the gourd.
Photograph by Kelly Hazel.

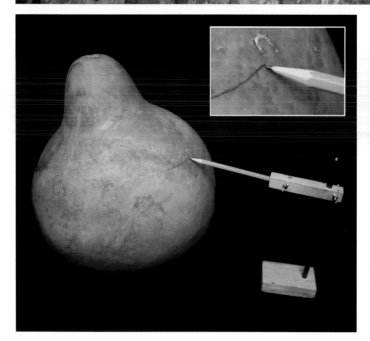

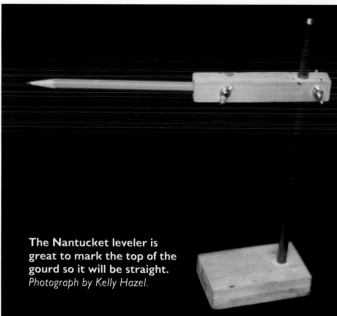

The Nantucket leveler is great to mark the top of the gourd so it will be straight.
Photograph by Kelly Hazel.

Marking and Cutting the Gourd

I like to place the spokes for my weaving in the top of the gourd after the top has been taken off (the flat surface of the cut gourd). You want the top to be level, so you need to mark where the gourd will be cut. I use a basket leveler. The leveler is used to mark Nantucket™ style basket rims so they are straight. The pencil in the top will mark the gourd as you turn it around. You could make one as it only takes some pieces of wood, or you can purchase it from a basket supplier.

Once the gourd has been marked, insert a knife on the line to make a space for the saw blade. You can also use a drill above the line to make a hole for the saw. Insert the saw blade and cut carefully on the line. You can use sandpaper afterwards to make the top nice and smooth. Now it is time to clean the inside of the gourd, so make sure you are using a mask!

Cleaning the Inside of the Gourd

Cleaning the inside of the gourd is important in order to have a professional looking piece of gourd art. A large metal spoon is a good tool to use in order to scrape the inside of the gourd. You can never tell what is inside the gourd until you open it up. The seed pouch may be intact or it could be open and all the seeds scattered around inside. Some gourds are very dry inside, but some may be damp and even have a terrible smell. Many times there will be stringy material or even a shiny white layer on the inside of the gourd that is hard to remove.

My husband Jim uses a wire brush designed to be attached to a drill chuck. They come in different sizes and different gauges. It depends on the condition of the inside of the gourd, but a 2" or 2-1/2" size brush usually works well. After using the brush, a hand sanding will make it look smooth and neat.

Karen Brown, another online friend, uses sanding balls to clean the insides of her gourds: "I clean a lot of gourds for my classes and the sanding balls and half cup titanium sanders work

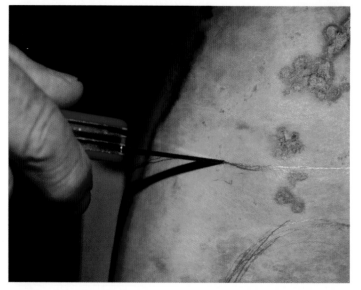

Insert a knife on the line and create an opening for the saw.
Photograph by Kelly Hazel.

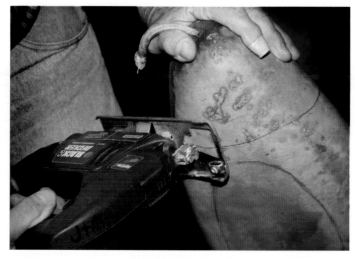

Insert the saw in the opening and cut the top of the gourd.
Photography by Kelly Hazel.

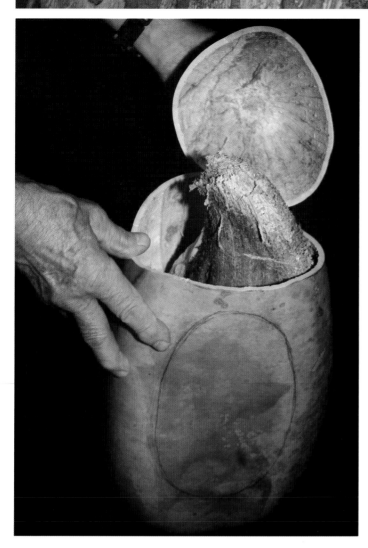

The inside of the gourd contains a seed sack. Sometimes it is open, but here it is intact. *Photography by Kelly Hazel.*

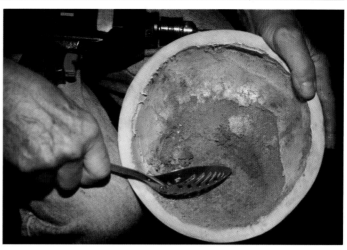

Jim uses a metal spoon to scrape out the seed before using the wire brush. *Photograph by Kelly Hazel.*

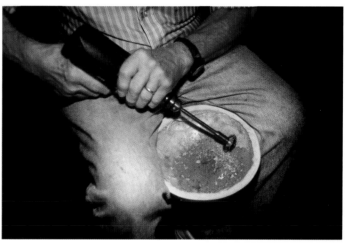

Jim uses a metal brush on his drill to finish cleaning the inside of the gourd. *Photography by Kelly Hazel.*

like magic for me. I have several of the ball sanders in different shaft lengths and grits. I attach them to the drill press and swing the plate around to the back to get it out of my way, put on a pair of rubber knobbed gloves and have at it. It makes short work of the mountain of gourds I usually have to clean all at once. For my own projects I then continue to sand the inside of the gourd with my 3-D sander until it's all smooth and polished."

There are several types of ball cleaners. One I would recommend is the carbide cleaner because they are tough and last a very long time. There is a mushroom shaped one, a donut shaped one, and a birdhouse/neck cleaner. They are on a heavy-duty 3/8" steel shaft that works on a regular drill shaft. Onno Bessigner from Guyton, Georgia, designed them.

"After taking pity on my poor arthritis-plagued wife I created these tools from a grinding head made of tungsten carbide. The tools are 8 inches long to make easy access to the gourd inner parts to clean and also prepare the gourd's membrane for removal in the case of a birdhouse. They are virtually indestructible and should last a lifetime!"

Some of the suppliers in the back of the book carry these gourd cleaners or you can order them directly from Onno. See the list of suppliers for more information.

Onno Bessigner from Guyton, Georgia, designed these gourd cleaners. *Photography by Derral Durrence.*

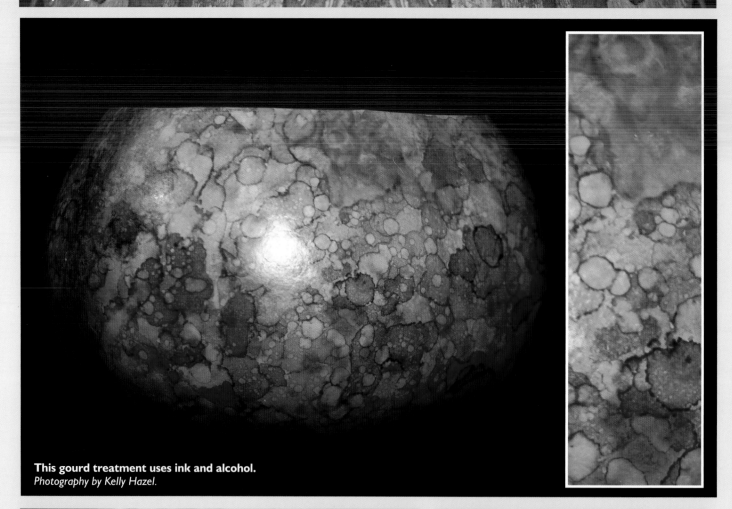

This gourd treatment uses ink and alcohol.
Photography by Kelly Hazel.

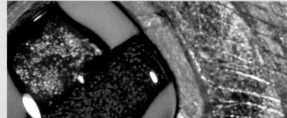

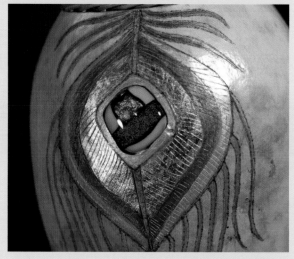

Woodburning and oil pencil decorate this gourd titled "Shells." *Photography by Kelly Hazel.*

The front of this gourd is decorated using dichroic glass, wood burning, and gold leafing. This gourd was done in a class taught by Bonnie Gibson of Arizona Gourds. *Photography by Dorothy Kozlowski.*

16

There are many ways to decorate a gourd before you weave, including painting, dyeing with inks and leather dye, decoupage, and spray paint. There are many things used to seal the gourd such as **UV resistant acrylic spray, wax, and varnish.** *Photography by Kelly Hazel.*

Finishing the Gourd

There are so many ways to finish the outside of the gourd. You can dye the gourd, paint it, woodburn designs on it, carve it, use colored or oil pencil on it, and draw with pen and ink on it. It is a wonderful versatile perfect pallet. Many times I use leather dye to decorate the gourd, but any technique is effective. You will see different techniques on the gourds in this book.

Drilling the Holes/Inserting the Spokes

You will be using round reed, also called rattan, for your spokes. Rattan, or cane palm, is a natural element. Rattan has been used in a wide variety of ways, including basket weaving for hundreds of years. Rattan is a vine that grows in the rain forests of many tropical countries in Asia. The core of the rattan is cut into different shapes and sizes called reeds and used for weaving. Reed is a very good weaving material mainly because it is lightweight, durable, and flexible. You can find more information on rattan in Flo Hoppe's book, *Wicker Basketry.*

As I said before, I like to use thick gourds so I can insert the spokes on top of the gourd. The pieces of reed used to make the frame for the basket are called "spokes." The ones you use for the actual weaving are called "weavers." The gourd needs to be at least 1/4" thick and flat on the top. Choose a drill bit that will make the hole the size to fit the reed spokes. I usually use a #3 round reed spoke, so I use a 5/64" or 1.98mm size drill bit. That makes the hole large enough, but still a little snug. If you have a very large basket, you may want to go to a #4 round reed spoke and a 3/32"

In order to place the spokes on top of the gourd, you need thick gourds. *Photography by Kelly Hazel.*

Angle the drill toward the outside of the gourd. *Photography by Kelly Hazel.*

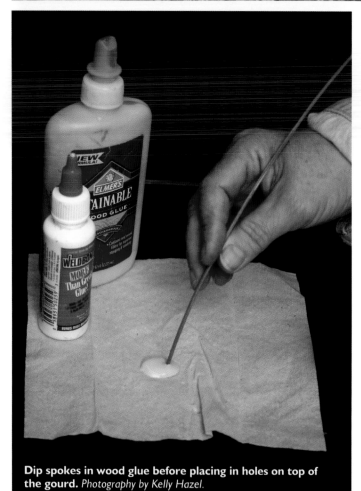

Dip spokes in wood glue before placing in holes on top of the gourd. *Photography by Kelly Hazel.*

Place spoke completely in the hole and then let it dry completely before weaving. *Photograph by Kelly Hazel.*

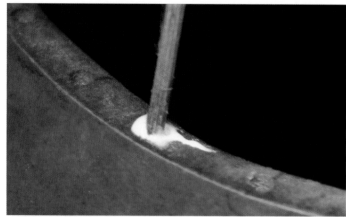

drill bit. Use a pencil and go around the flat top of the gourd, marking it every 1/2". Tilt the drill at a slight angle with the tip of the drill angling toward the front of the gourd. You can see this in the picture. Drill about 1/4" deep (deeper if it is a really thick gourd). Try not to drill outside the front or the inside of the gourd. Sometimes it will happen no matter how careful you think you are drilling, but don't worry — it's a quick fix. I just take some of the dust from the gourd, mix it with white glue, and plug the hole. Make sure you smooth it on the surface. Using the gourd dust will make it the same color as the gourd and it will accept staining. Cut your pieces of #3 or #4 round reeds long enough to make the weaving as tall as you want. Just remember to leave about three or four inches for making the rim. The rim is the finished top of the gourd and keeps it from coming unwoven. For an 8" diameter gourd I usually cut my spokes around fourteen inches long. I will have specific lengths and the number of spokes you will need in the patterns. Some weaving techniques will need a specific number of spokes to create the pattern in the weaving.

Now you are ready to insert the spokes in the hole. Do not wet the spokes at this point. You may get some pieces that are a little larger and do not want to fit in the hole. If that is the case, just use your scissors or nippers and cut the end of the spoke at an angle. I also use wood glue to glue the spokes in until I have some weaving in place. I make a puddle

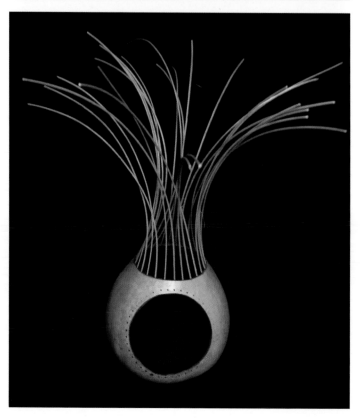

Let the spokes curve outward so the weaving will not get so tight. *Photography by Kelly Hazel.*

18

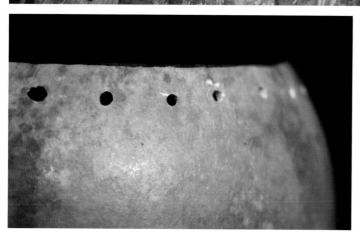

Sometimes when the gourd is not thick, the holes will need to be drilled on the sides. *Photography by Kelly Hazel.*

Flatten the pinched area on the inside of the gourd. *Photography by Kelly Hazel.*

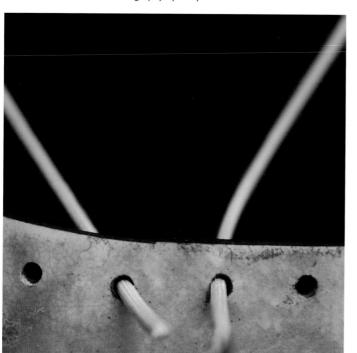

Step one is to place the ends of the reed from inside to outside. *Photography by Kelly Hazel.*

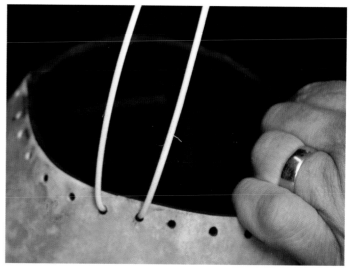

Pull reed up to make two spokes. *Photography by Kelly Hazel.*

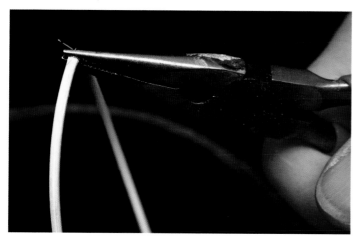

Pinch the center of the reed spoke with needle nose pliers to break fibers. *Photography by Kelly Hazel.*

of glue and dip the end in it before inserting it into the hole. Always have the bend of the spoke going outward. It is very easy to weave tight and make your basket go in too much. The spokes need to stay an even distance apart, so by inserting the spokes with the curve going outward, it helps to keep the basket from getting too small in diameter as you weave. After inserting the spokes, let them dry before wetting them.

If you have a gourd that is not thick enough to put the spokes on the top, you can still weave on it. The spokes will just be inserted differently. Make your spokes twice the length that you would for a spoke going on top of the gourd. Drill your holes around the side of the gourd, 1/4" down from the top and 1/2" apart. You will need to wet your spokes since we will be bending them. Fold your spoke in half and gently use needle nose pliers to break the fibers. From the inside of the gourd place one end of the spoke through one hole and the other end through the very next hole. Pull both ends gently through the holes to the outside with the bend in the center. Flatten the bend against the inside of the gourd. Do this with each spoke. If you have an uneven number of holes, cut a spoke in half and insert one end inside the gourd behind a loop made by the bent part of the last spoke. Then pull the other end through the last hole to the outside of the gourd.

Pods, shells, and pine cones can be used for embellishments. *Photography by Kelly Hazel.*

Birch bark and cedar bark strips. *Photography by Kelly Hazel.*

Natural and dyed cane. *Photography by Kelly Hazel.*

Seagrass, mohair, and yarn used in the undulating tapestry gourd weaving. *Photography by Kelly Hazel.*

 # 2 round reed for weavers and #3 round reed for spokes. *Photography by Kelly Hazel.*

20

Gathering Your Weaving Materials

This is the part of preparing to weave that I really love. The materials you select will create the design in the weaving. For the undulating weaving you will want to use materials with texture. Cass Schorsch introduced me to using bark in my weaving. In the class that I took with her we used the inner layer of western red cedar bark, red pine bark, and yellow pine bark. I have also used Alaskan yellow cedar, birch bark, and hickory bark. Cedar has been gathered for hundreds of years and used for weaving. The inner layer of cedar bark was carefully removed from the tree, by making a horizontal cut in the bark. The soft inner bark was separated, rolled up and hung to dry. When dry, the bark was cut into strips to be used for weaving. Harvesting and uses of bark by the Native Americans are found in the book, *Cedar: Tree of Life to the Northwest Coast Indians* written by Hillary Stewart. Cedar bark can be ordered online either in large chunks or already prepared and cut into strips. You will need to soak the prepared bark strips for at least half an hour before weaving, as it needs to be pliable.

Other materials I like to use are round reed, yarns, mohair, sisal, waxed linen thread, coir (coconut hair), sweet grass, leather, vines, and wire — just about anything that can be bent and woven. You can also collect grasses, day lily and iris stems, and braid them into a cordage to be woven into the basket. Many times I will weave or use as decorations materials from Florida. I have friends who will gather these items for me or I will gather them when I visit. Philodendron plants grow large in Florida. When a new leaf emerges, it casts off the sheath. This sheath can be gathered, soaked, and woven into the basket or used as a cover for the rim. Palm stems can also be soaked and woven. I also use jacaranda pods that grow on trees in Florida for embellishments.

The varieties, textures, and colors of materials that can be used in baskets are endless. Don't be afraid to try and weave different materials. That is what makes weaving fun! There are several good books on gathering and preparing natural materials for weaving. One is *Natural Baskets* by Maryanne Gillooly. This book has a chapter on bark basketry by Cass Schorsch. Another book, *From Vines to Vessels* by Beryl Omega Lumpkin, has information on identifying, gathering and preparing many different natural materials such as grapevines, honeysuckle, willow, wisteria, barks, cattails, pine needles, grasses, and even kudzu. In my home library I have many books that have been valuable sources of information for my weaving and gathering of materials, both for baskets and gourds. I have a list of books that I use in the bibliography.

Dyeing Materials

There are many different kinds of dyes, both natural and chemical. You can even use walnut hulls to make a basket dye. I will describe my method of dyeing materials, although there are several different ways of doing it. I have large tubs that I fill with boiling water. I put in the amount of dye that will make the color dark enough for me, and then dip in the material. If I want the material darker, I just leave in for a longer time. Some materials like paper cording you can only dip and remove, but reed and seagrass rope can be left in the dye for short periods of time. Seagrass rope is made from natural seagrass that has been twisted together. For reed and seagrass, after the dye bath I rinse in vinegar water. I just put a capful of white vinegar in a tub of clear cold water. Then put the dyed material on newspapers to dry. Placing the dyed materials outdoors to dry is best. I use either Rit® dye or Jacquard® dyes made for basket reed.

Natural and dyed reed for spokes and weavers. *Photography by Kelly Hazel.*

Philodendron sheath. *Photography by Kelly Hazel.*

Chapter Three:

Weaving Techniques

This chapter covers the various techniques used in the projects found in this book. You can vary these techniques and use different ones in the same gourd basket and be able to make hundreds of different baskets just by the techniques, colors, and materials you use. You will cover the simple weave, twine, triple twine, increasing and decreasing, and twills. I have chosen techniques and projects that even a beginner can do. The instructions I use are for a right-handed person as I am right handed. If you are left-handed, just reverse the direction.

Simple Weave

Simple weave, also called in-and-out, over-and-under, plain weave, or randing, is the easiest weave to do. You can use flat materials like flat reed or bark or round materials like round reed or seagrass. The spokes will show through this weaving technique, so using different color spokes and weavers can create interest. This weave is also used for the turn backs or decreasing and increasing that I use in the undulating basket. These techniques will be explained later.

If you want to use the simple weave all the way around the basket, you will need an uneven number of spokes. You will take the weaver behind a spoke, in front of a spoke, and repeat that all the way around the basket. When you return to the beginning, you will continue, but will weave on top of the last row. The second row will be just the opposite. The

spoke that had the weaver behind it will now have the weaver in front, and the spoke that had the weaver in front of it will now have the weaver behind it. This alternating pattern will be evident each row you weave.

If the pattern calls for an even number of spokes you will need to compensate if there are any areas of continuous simple weave. You will have this happen when you weave rows of barks or leather in an undulating gourd basket. The pattern for this is in the projects chapter. Gourds are different sizes and will end up with different numbers of spokes. You will compensate by weaving behind one spoke, in front of one spoke, all the way around the basket. If you have an even number of spokes, when you get back to the beginning it will not naturally create an alternating pattern. You will make it do this by either going behind two spokes or in front of two spokes to get back to the original pattern of behind one spoke, in front of one spoke. You will have to do this after every row, but it will move over in a different place every time. This will create a spiraling pattern and looks good in the design.

You can vary your simple weave design by using two or three weavers as one and go behind one spoke and in front of the next one. Using different colored weavers will also vary the pattern. You can use this one weaving technique for an entire gourd basket and by varying the number of weavers or the color of the weavers you can create many different looking gourd baskets.

Simple weave. *Photography by Kelly Hazel.*

Weaving with cedar bark in an over and under pattern. *Photography by Kelly Hazel.*

22

Twining

The next technique is called twining or pairing weave. You use two weavers for this technique. They can both be the same color or for a variation use two different colors. Mark two corresponding spokes with a ribbon or twist tie or just bend down a small piece of the spoke at the top. Place the end of one weaver behind the first marked spoke and the end of the second weaver behind the second marked spoke. Take the first weaver (the left one) and bring it in front of the next spoke and over the second weaver, and behind the second spoke going to the right and then bring the weaver out. The second weaver is now on the left. Pick it up and repeat what you just did with the first weaver. You will continue this pattern, always beginning with the left weaver. The two weavers twist together between the spokes. This locks them in place and creates a very strong sturdy weave.

Illustration of twining. *Scanned by Kelly Hazel.*

Place two weavers behind two consecutive spokes. *Photography by Kelly Hazel.*

The weavers twist around the spokes. *Photography by Kelly Hazel.*

Triple Twine and a Step-Up

Triple twine or three-rod wale is one of my favorite weaving techniques using round reed. Since you are using three weavers, you can vary the look of the weaving just by using different colors of weavers and spokes. This weave will make your weaving very strong and sturdy. It locks everything in place. In my undulating gourd basket, I use different types of weaving going up the basket in layers. I use a single row of triple twine weave between each layer to lock everything in place, pack all the material down so there will be no holes in the weaving, and make the entire basket very sturdy. In a basket woven entirely of round reed, you can create arrows, darts, spiraling, and many other designs just by using triple twine weaving and varying the colors in the weavers. You will see this in the project, "Triple Twine Gourd Basket with Spiraling and Arrow."

Mark three consecutive spokes with ribbon or twist ties. I usually just bend down the first spoke at the top about 1/4". In the triple twine technique you will need to know where

the beginning spoke is located. Since you do have to add to the weavers when they run out, you will have a hard time finding the beginning spoke just by looking inside the basket. Place the three weavers behind each marked spoke.

Take the weaver that is behind the first marked spoke to the left. It goes in front of the next two spokes, over the next two weavers, behind the next third spoke, and out again. Now pick up the second weaver, which is now the first weaver to the left. Repeat the same sequence you did with the first weaver: in front of two spokes, over the two weavers, behind the next spoke, and out. This sequence will continue all the way around the gourd basket. Remember to always start with the first weaver to the left and move to the right each time. The way the rows will end is determined by the pattern you are using. If you are using the triple twine for a narrow area in the basket and want the rows to be exactly on top of each other or if you are making arrows, you will need to do a step-up technique at the end of each row. If you want a spiraling effect, you will not use the step-up.

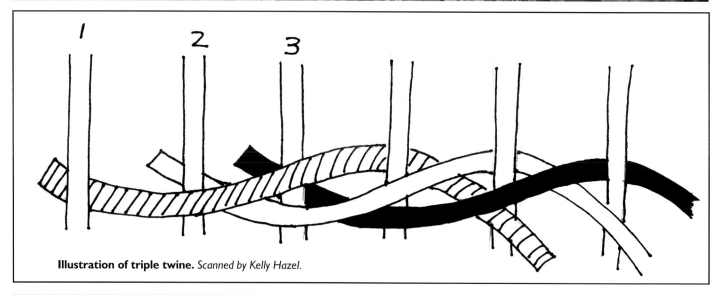

Illustration of triple twine. *Scanned by Kelly Hazel.*

Triple twine uses three weavers. *Photography by Kelly Hazel.*

First weaver moves right and goes in front of two spokes and behind the next. *Photography by Kelly Hazel.*

Second weaver goes to the right in front of two spokes and behind the next. *Photography by Kelly Hazel.*

Third weaver moves to the right, going over two spokes and behind the next. *Photography by Kelly Hazel.*

Step-Up

Once you learn the triple twine technique, the step-up should be easy. You will only do it at the end of each row. It is used to place each row directly on top of each other. It is three steps that are the reverse of the triple twine technique. Weave until you reach the first marked spoke, stop weaving at the spoke just before the first marked spoke.

- **Step One**: Take the last weaver on the right. It will go in front of the next two corresponding spokes to the right, behind the next spoke and out.

- **Step Two**: Take the weaver in the middle. It will go in front of the next two corresponding spokes to the right, behind the next spoke, and out.

- **Step Three**: Take the weaver on the left. It will go in front of two corresponding spokes to the right, behind the next, and out. You are actually going backwards until you reach the very first marked spoke. This makes a complete row of triple twine and places you exactly in the same place you began the row. The step-up will be done after every row.

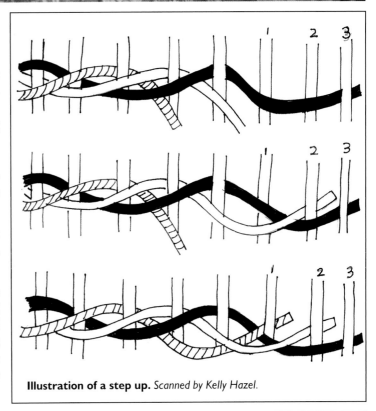

Illustration of a step up. *Scanned by Kelly Hazel.*

Third weaver goes over two spokes to the right and under the next. *Photography by Kelly Hazel.*

Second weaver goes over two spokes and behind the next. *Photography by Kelly Hazel.*

First weaver goes over two spokes and behind the next. *Photography by Kelly Hazel.*

Finished row. *Photography by Kelly Hazel.*

Increasing and Decreasing

I use increasing and decreasing in my undulating gourd basket. I also call them hills and valleys. I like to weave a landscape in this gourd basket. The different materials will look different in this technique. This is where soft materials like yarns, mohair, and seagrass rope can be used to create the texture. Since I build this basket in layers, I use triple twine between the layers. This packs the soft material down. If you are using yarn or mohair, you will want to use three or four strands as one. Weave twice the rows you would with hard material like the seagrass or round reed.

To begin, decide where you want to build a hill; you will use a simple weave to do this. This will start the first layer. Determine how wide you want your hill to be. The wider the space, the taller the hill will be. I usually weave three or four hills around the basket, depending on the size of the gourd. Take the end of the material (weaver) and place it behind a spoke and simple weave to the right to the place your hill will end. Bring the weaver around that last spoke and simple weave backwards to the left toward the beginning spoke. Stop

Increasing and decreasing to create hills and valleys. *Scanned by Kelly Hazel.*

one spoke before you get to the beginning spoke, go around that spoke and weave back to the right. You will decrease one spoke on each side until you only have two spokes left. You will then turn on that spoke and go all the way back to the last spoke you went around. Go one more spoke past that one, turn around and go all the way to the end and finish the hill one spoke past the end. Cut the weaver and put it to the inside of the basket. This builds a hill and ends it so that the weaving is even. Move somewhere else on the basket and start another hill. There are two rules when weaving hills. The first one is to never begin or end your hill on the same spoke. The second rule is never to have two consecutive rows with turn backs on the same spoke. This will create gaps in your weaving. If you are using fluffy yarns you will hide this gap, but with reed or seagrass, you will see the gap and it will take away from the appearance of the weaving. After you feel confident making the hills, you can try some variations. You can weave half a hill, turn around and go back and start again. Experiment and see how many different patterns you can make. Experiment with the types of materials you are using as well.

After making your hills, you will weave one row of triple twine and then end with a step-up. This will lock in your first layer and all the materials you used. Pack the triple twine row tight against the hills so there are no gaps in the weaving. Now you will see the valleys. You will need to fill in the valleys to make your weaving level again. This time you will start at the bottom of the valley; go back and forth across the spokes increasing one spoke each time on each side until you fill in the areas.

Completed hills. *Photography by Dorothy Kozlowski.*

1

Begin the hills by looping the weaver around a spoke. *Photography by Kelly Hazel.*

2

Every time you go across the area with simple weave, decrease a spoke. *Photography by Kelly Hazel.*

3

Continue until you only have two spokes left. *Photography by Kelly Hazel.*

4

Then go all the way to the end of the hill, one spoke past the last one and turn around on that spoke. *Photography by Kelly Hazel.*

5

End the hill on the other side, one spoke past. *Photography by Kelly Hazel.*

Twills

Let's start with a simple explanation of a twill technique: a twill is a pattern or design in a basket where instead of just going over one under one (simple weave) you go over different numbers of spokes in the same basket. The pattern in this book is for a continuous twill weave. If a continuous twill weave is woven in one direction, you will see the pattern, as it will spiral around the basket. The twill design will really stand out if color is used, either with dyed spokes or dyed weavers. With all twill baskets you must determine the number of spokes to be used in order to create the pattern. In the project pattern in this book, you will weave over two spokes and under two spokes all the way around the basket in continuous twill weave. Sandy Roback is a basket maker, and she has written her explanation of how she determines the number of spokes for a continuous twill weave in a basket. You can also apply this to a woven basket on a gourd.

Twill basket. *Photography by Dorothy Kozlowski.*

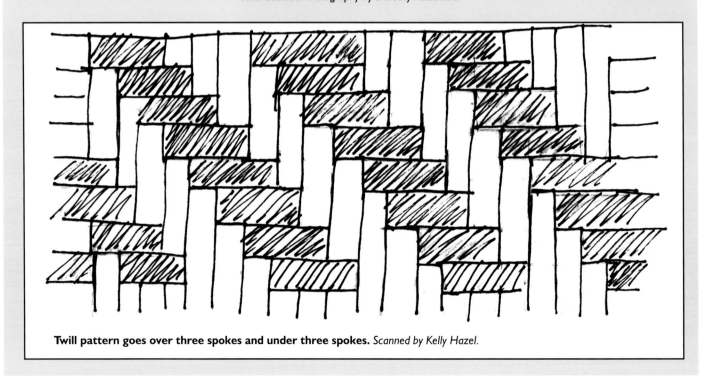

Twill pattern goes over three spokes and under three spokes. *Scanned by Kelly Hazel.*

Creating a Continuous Twill

Continuous twills are based on a repeat numerical pattern, meaning the same thing happens again and again. Continuous twills are woven using only one weaver and will automatically "step up" when you come back to the starting point.

In my basket, you see a "pattern" of 7 (as in under 1 – over 1 – under 2 – over 3). In order to make the pattern continuous, the number of spokes must equal the pattern (7) plus or minus one. On a round slotted base you can use any multiple of 7 plus or minus one. For example:

- 22 spokes (21+1)

- 34 spokes (35-1)

- 36 spokes (35+1)

This will create the 1-2-3 twill.

To create a square base basket (like the cathead), the math is a little different. This pattern of 7 requires a multiple of 7 plus or minus one, but the number of spokes must also be divided by 4. Examples:

- 7x5 = 35+1 = 36 divided by 4 = 9 (9x9 base)

- 7x7 = 49-1 = 48 divided by 4 = 12 (12x12 base)

- 7x9 = 63+1 = 64 divided by 4 = 16 (16x16 base)

You can see the pattern of the 1-2-3 twill in Sandy's basket.
Photography by Dorothy Kozlowski.

Creating your twill basket using this method means you do not need to add a spoke in a corner like you might do in some baskets where you want a continuous weave rather than a chase weave or a stop/start. Usually the spokes are dyed and the weaver is plain because the design shows clearer but you can also do the reverse or have both elements plain. This system will work any continuous twill weave, just pay attention to the numbers.

Color enhances the twill pattern. *Photography by Dorothy Kozlowski.*

Chapter Four:

Projects

The following projects are ones that a beginner or experienced weaver should be able to make. Refer to *Chapter Two* to learn how to prepare the gourd and *Chapter Three* to learn about the weaving techniques as you make the project. *Chapter Five* shows different borders you can use and *Chapter Six* provides ideas for adding embellishments to the finished woven gourd.

All of the projects are for weaving on gourds. Be sure and soak your reed for a few minutes before using. Cedar bark and philodendron sheath need to be soaked for forty-five minutes to an hour. Keep spokes and weavers wet at all times. I use a spray bottle and spray often. Do not let water collect inside your gourd, so spray with the gourd upside down.

Twine and Triple Twine Woven Gourd

This gourd basket is an easy one to learn twine and triple twine. Prepare the gourd with any number of spokes. You can use different colors and different numbers of rows to create many different baskets.

Materials

- Thick gourd
- #3 round reed for spokes (dyed or natural or smoked)
- #2 round reed for weavers (blue and mauve)
- Dyed seagrass rope – mini size in blue and mauve
- Philodendron sheath
- Waxed linen thread
- Needle
- Pods and beads for decorations
- Wood glue
- Spray bottle, bucket, and water for soaking materials
- Drill
- Saw
- Cleaning supplies to clean gourd

Weaving the Basket

You will begin by using the triple twine technique. You will twine for three rows and then weave a step up at the end. You will be using two #2 round reed weavers of blue and one weaver of mauve. Keep your spokes wet by spraying them often! Next you will use two pieces of the blue seagrass rope and twine for three rows. Weave one row of triple twine with two pieces of blue and one of mauve #2 round reed and weave a step up at the end. This will divide the area of twined seagrass. Then you will twine three rows of mauve seagrass. The final weaving will be six rows of triple twine with two #2 round reed mauve weavers and one blue weaver. End with a step-up. Now we are ready for the border.

The Border

Wet the spokes well as they will be used to make the border. If the spokes are not thoroughly wet, they will break. I usually put my spokes upside down in a bucket of water for a while. We will end with a simple braided border and cover it with philodendron sheath. You will learn how to do this in *Chapter Five*. You can also add pods and beads as embellishments.

Opposite, Clockwise from top left:

Marianne's twine and triple twine gourd basket. *Photography by Dorothy Kozlowski.*

This basket ends with a covered rim. *Photography by Dorothy Kozlowski.*

In Betsey Sloan's basket, you can clearly see the sections of twining. *Photography by Kelly Hazel.*

Triple Twine Gourd with Spiraling and Arrow

This is a fun basket using round reed. You can do variations of this using different colors and placing the spirals and arrows in different places.

Materials

- #3 round reed for spokes (I used chocolate brown)
- #2 round reed for weavers in three different colors (red, yellow, orange)
- Medium size gourd – around seven or eight inches diameter
- Pods and beads for decoration (optional)
- Wood glue
- Drill
- Saw
- Cleaning supplies
- Spray bottle, bucket, and water for soaking materials

Preparation

Prepare the gourd using either a thick gourd with spokes in the top or a thinner gourd with spokes around the sides. The spoke number needs to be divisible by three minus one. Examples are 23, 26, 29, 32, etc. I used thirty-two chocolate brown spokes that were glued in holes drilled on top of the gourd.

Weaving the Basket

Mark the first spoke you put your weavers behind. Weave five rows of triple twine using the red reed weavers. Do not weave a step up. Remember to keep your weavers and spokes wet by spraying them often. When you get to the beginning spoke, cut the red weaver and replace it with a yellow weaver. You will leave a two-inch tail on the red weaver and place it behind the spokes. Add the new yellow weaver in the same place. Continue to triple twine weave for four rows with two red and one yellow weaver. At the end of the fourth row, cut the next red weaver and add another yellow weaver. Triple twine for four rows with one red and two yellow weavers. When you finish the four rows and get back to the beginning marked spoke, cut the last red weaver and add the last yellow weaver. Triple twine three rows with three yellow weavers. End by placing all the ends of the weavers behind the spokes and cut them. Leave them long enough to stay caught behind the spokes. You are ready to make an arrow.

Now, take three orange weavers. Triple twine all the way around the gourd for one row and end at the spoke before the marked one. Do a step up, cut the spokes, and tuck them behind to the inside of the gourd. Cut three more orange weavers. Insert them the opposite direction using the same marked spokes. Weave one row of triple twine backwards to the left and end at the spoke before the marked spoke; then do a step up. These two rows create an arrow. Now it is time for the rim.

The Rim

You can use a simple braided border or a variation. I used the second variation in this basket. You will find it in *Chapter Five*. Be sure and wet your spokes well before beginning your rim.

Close up of an arrow. *Photography by Kelly Hazel.*

Rim is a variation of the simple rolled border. *Photography by Kelly Hazel.*

**The author's basket, "Shells," is an example of triple twine
with spiraling and an arrow.** *Photography by Kelly Hazel.*

33

Gourd Basket with Four Rod Wale

Terry and John Noxel from Pennsylvania created this basket. They also wrote the following pattern. They are active members of the Pennsylvania Gourd Society. The design is developed by using four rod wale on spokes divisible by four, plus one. Four rod wale is just like triple twine except that you use four weavers instead of three.

Materials

- Tall and thick gourd; cut in half the length of the gourd
- Sand the gourd inside and out, and finish both surfaces (the interior of this one was flocked, the outside was sanded to a sheen and rubbed with bowling alley wax)
- Yellow basket dye (color one)
- Black basket dye (color two)
- #3 round reed
- 1/4" drill bit
- Elmer's wood glue®

Directions

Dye the reed according to the manufacturer's directions. Measure the circumference of the gourd in inches, and double that number. Determine closest number divisible by four, and add one. In this case the circumference was twenty-seven inches. 27 x 2 is 54, but 54 was not divisible by four, but 52 was. I added one (52 plus one), and marked 53 spokes approximately 1/2" apart. Use a pencil and place a mark 1/2" apart around the rim of the gourd. Using 1/4" drill bit, drill vertically for each spoke (depth about 1/4"). Cut 14" spokes from color one. Glue spokes into drilled holes and let dry. Weave a four rod wale to the right for six rows using three black and one yellow weaver.

Four rod wale is as follows: mark the starting point and weave each weaver in front of two spokes, behind two spokes, and out. Do this for six rows. After six rows, cut weavers and tuck down on the right side of spoke to spoke. Take four new weavers of the same colors and tuck in the same place. It will be a very tight fit. Weave four rod wale to the left for six rows. After six rows cut weavers and tuck down to the right of the spoke. Using the spokes weave a double border (behind two spokes, in front of two spokes, and down to the front/in). Let work dry overnight, then trim off weavers inside of weaving.

Gourd Basket With Four Rod Wale. *Courtesy of Terry and John Noxel.*

Inside of the gourd.
Courtesy of Terry and John Noxel.

Undulating Tapestry Gourd Weave

Materials

- #3 round reed or smoked reed for spokes
- #2 round reed for weavers (space dyed, dyed different colors, or natural)
- Dyed seagrass (I used natural, blue, and yellow in this gourd)
- Different kinds and colors of yarn and mohair
- Cedar bark
- Philodendron sheath
- Waxed linen thread
- Tapestry Needle
- Pods and beads for decoration
- Wood glue
- Drill
- Saw
- Cleaning supplies
- Scissors
- Spray bottle, bucket, and water for soaking materials

You can see the hills and valleys in this tapestry gourd. *Photography by Kelly Hazel.*

Weaving the Basket

I used two pieces of tan #2 round reed and one piece of brown #2 round reed for weavers. Soak them for several minutes. Triple twine for two to three rows. You can end with a step up or not. Begin a tapestry (undulating) weave by using mini seagrass. I started with blue seagrass. You will be making hills and valleys. You do this by weaving small areas and making turn backs in order to form the hills. This is called increasing and decreasing. This technique is discussed in chapter four. Make two to four hills around your gourd. The number will depend on the size of your gourd. Then I add the row of distinction. This is one row of triple twine. Then push everything down so you will have no gaps in your weaving. Now, fill in the valleys and build more hills. You can use seagrass or yarns. Weave the row of distinction. Now you can weave several rows of cedar bark. The cedar bark needs to be soaked for at least forty-five minutes before weaving. You will need to taper one end of the bark. Place it behind one spoke, in front of the next all the way around the basket. This is called simple weave. You will be using a continuous weave. Weave three or four rows. Then make another layer of hills and valleys. End the weaving with four rows of triple twine. This gourd can have the border exposed or covered with a philodendron sheath. In this gourd I wove a row of philodendron sheath and then several rows of triple twine. Then I ended with an exposed simple braided border.

This example of an undulating tapestry gourd was made by the author. *Photography by Dorothy Kozlowski.*

An undulating tapestry gourd, "Swimming with the Dolphins."

Continuous Twill Woven Gourd

Materials

- Thick gourd
- #3 round reed for spokes (dyed, smoked, or natural)
- #2 round reed for weavers (dyed or natural)
- Medium Bleached Hamburg Cane (dyed or natural)
- Philodendron sheath
- Waxed linen thread
- Tapestry Needle
- Pods and beads for decoration
- Wood glue
- Drill
- Saw
- Cleaning supplies
- Spray bottle, bucket, and water for soaking materials

Weaving the Basket

Prepare your gourd and materials. In this basket I used a continuous woven twill basket based on a pattern of four (under two, over two). You will use increments of four (20, 24, 28, 32, 36, and 40, plus or minus one). I cut nineteen space dyed spokes around fourteen inches long. The first two

The twill pattern can be seen in this basket made and photographed by the author, "Rust."

rows are triple twine using space dyed reed and the weavers are natural medium Hamburg cane®. Taper the end of the cane and weave under two spokes, over two spokes all the way around the gourd. The next row will go on top of the first. Continue this for twenty-five rows. Taper the end and weave in about where the twill was started. This will make your basket level. Then triple twine for four to five rows; cut weavers and tuck behind the beginning spokes. Make a simple border going behind two spokes and down on the first step and in front of two spokes and in on the second step. Clip spokes on the inside and cover with philodendron sheath. You can see how to do this in *Chapter Five*.

To start the twill, place the tapered end behind a few spokes.

Once you weave a few rows, you will begin to see the twill pattern.

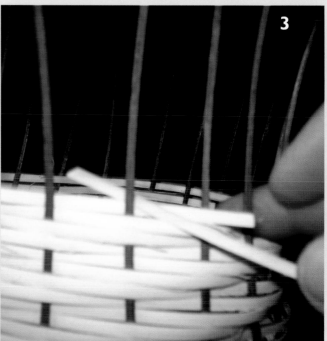

If your weaver ends, add a new one on top of the old and weave together a few spokes to secure.

"Emerald," by the author, is a twill woven gourd. *Photography by Dorothy Kozlowski.*

Chapter Five:

The Rim

The rim is what secures the basket together. It is the finished top of the basket. In a gourd basket it is usually made by interweaving the spokes. The rim makes the entire basket strong and secure. The following are borders that I use in my gourd baskets. There are a few that can be used with or without a basket.

Simple Rolled Border

and Variations

The simple rolled border looks very nice on a gourd basket. It is strong and very easy to weave. If you look at the photographs in sequence you will see how easy it is to do. You actually use the spokes to make the border. Soak your spokes well. Running them under warm water or placing upside down in a bucket of water for about five minutes should help. If you have been spraying your spokes throughout the entire weaving process, the spokes should be wet enough. You do not need to wet the weavers or inside the gourd, just the base

This is a four step simple rolled border. *Photography by Dorothy Kozlowski.*

A border covered with philodendron sheath. *Photography by Dorothy Kozlowski.*

40

Step one is to go behind two spokes and down. *Photography by Kelly Hazel.*

Do this all the way around the gourd. *Photography by Kelly Hazel.*

of the spokes where you will be bending them. You can use a needle nose pliers and pinch them close to the weaving. This will help, because you just do not want to break the spokes in case you want them to show and not be covered with philodendron sheath.

Take any three spokes. You will be moving to the right. Place the spoke to the left behind the two to the right and down to the front of the basket. Pick up a new spoke to have three and repeat this sequence. Continue this weaving all the way around the gourd.

When you have only two spokes left, loosen the first loop to the right and put the left spoke through it. Then loosen the second loop to the right and put the last spoke through it. Tighten both loops to finish the first step.

When you only have two spokes left, push up the loop formed by the first spoke. *Photography by Kelly Hazel.*

Place next to last spoke through the hole. *Photography by Kelly Hazel.*

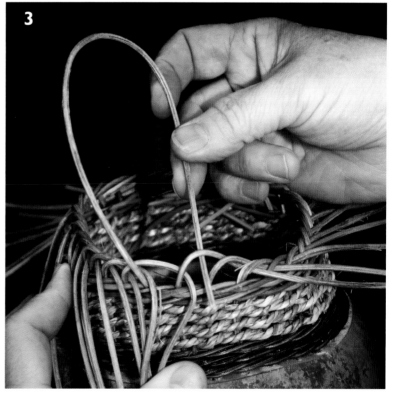

Last spoke goes through hole made by the second spoke. *Photography by Kelly Hazel.*

41

The next step is to go over two spokes that are sticking out the front and then go inside the basket through the hole made by the first row. This hole is right beside the third spoke to the right. Continue all the way around until you have two spokes left. Pull the first two spokes out a little and place the last two spokes through those holes. Tighten the loops just like in the first step.

The last step (opposite page) will be used if you decide to leave the border uncovered. This step will hide the ending spokes and make the basket look neater. You now have all your spokes to the inside. If they are still long you can cut some off, but be careful that you have enough to weave. Take three spokes in your hand. Bring them straight out. Place one spoke on top of two spokes to the right and down. Continue this all the way around the basket. Finish the way you did the other two steps. Let the reed dry and then you can cut off the ends so they will be hidden behind the last row. So in review: step one is behind two and down, step two is in front of two and in, and step three is on top of two and down.

Squeeze rim to tighten all spokes. *Photography by Kelly Hazel.*

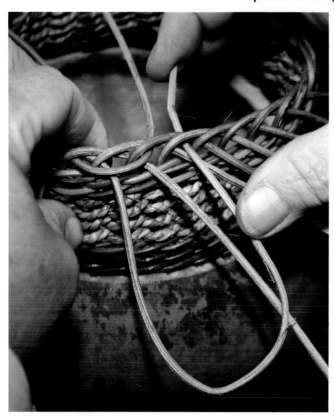

Step two is to take the spokes over two and through to the inside of the gourd. *Photography by Kelly Hazel.*

Last two spokes goes through the holes made by the first two spokes to the inside of the gourd. *Photography by Kelly Hazel.*

42

Step three is to do the same thing on the inside that you did in step one: over two and down. *Photography by Kelly Hazel.*

All the way around the gourd. *Photography by Kelly Hazel.*

When the spokes are dry, cut them and tuck under the last row you wove. *Photography by Kelly Hazel.*

You can vary the rolled border by adding or eliminating steps. If you are covering your border with something like philodendron sheath, you can eliminate step three, because the ends will not show. So it will be behind two and down, over two and in, then cut the spokes. The following are other variations you can use: Behind two and down, hold the spokes out and go on top of two and down, in front of two and in, over two and down, cut the spokes; in front of two and in, over two and down, cut the spokes.

A variation of the rolled border is the Japanese braid border. In this border you use two spokes instead of two. Do not use the pliers to pinch, as you want the braid to be rounded. You will use two spokes behind two spokes and down all the way around, then two spokes in front of two spokes and in. You can use two or three steps. Just follow the same steps you used in the rolled border. So you see there are many variations. Don't be afraid to experiment.

The finished rim. *Photography by Kelly Hazel.*

Debbie Wilson did a simple braided border using two spokes at a time in this gourd basket. *Photography by Dorothy Kozlowski.*

Covered Rim

The covered rim works well with the Undulating Tapestry Gourd Basket. I use philodendron sheath from Florida to cover my rims. Soak the sheath for forty-five minutes to an hour before using. I weave a two-step simple rolled border first, then open the sheath and lay it around the rim. You can use one to three sheaths to cover. I place the longest one all the way around the gourd. The other sheath tails can be cut short and placed under the longest sheath. You can use clothespins to secure the sheaths to the rim. Thread a needle with waxed linen thread. Usually three times around the gourd will be long enough. Leave one end short. Start under the head of the sheath and stitch away from the heads. Stitch from the front, just under the sheath, and go through to the inside. Leave a tail. Come back around to the front. Catch the tail that is hanging and stitch it under the sheath. Pull stitches tight. Move over about an inch. Go from the front to the back, around to the front again. Pull tightly. Keep going all the way around the rim. When you get back to the philodendron sheath head, come through the head. Add an embellishment, if desired, and stitch back to the inside, and tie it off.

Border covered with philodendron sheath. *Photography by Dorothy Kozlowski.*

End the stitching and add a decoration like a jacaranda pod. *Photography by Kelly Hazel.*

Maxine Riley used a philodendron sheath for her rim.
Photography by Dorothy Kozlowski.

More than one sheath can be used. *Photography by Dorothy Kozlowski.*

Gretchen Rim

This rim can be used on top of weaving or alone as a woven decorated border. If it is on top of the weaving you will be using the spokes to weave the border, so when you cut spokes for the basket, make sure you cut them long enough. The pattern below, submitted by Charlotte Durrence, is done directly on top of the gourd.

Materials

- #2 round reed
- Gourd bowl about six to seven inches at the top
- Awl or drill
- Spray bottle, bucket, and water for soaking materials
- Sharp scissors

Directions

Prepare and cut the gourd as a bowl. Make sure the top of the gourd is straight. You will need to drill holes about 1/4" down from the top and about 1/2" apart. Use a 3/32" bit or be sure the holes will accommodate the #2 reed. Also be sure you have an even number of holes. Count the holes and cut half that many reeds. Cut the #2 reed in five feet lengths. It is important to soak the reed in water and continue to spray with water as you work with it. Put the ends of the reed together making a hairpin shape. Insert the two ends into two of the holes on the bowl from the outside to the inside. Continue doing this until all of the reeds

How to insert spokes. *Photography by Derral Durrence.*

"Gretchen Rim" by Charlotte Durrence.
Photography by Derral Durrence.

have been inserted. Pick up three of the reeds. Bring the left reed around behind the other two reeds and pull it out and down. Pick up another reed on the right side. Again take the left reed and put it around behind the other two reeds and pull it out and down. Continue this until you are all the way around the gourd bowl. You will have two reeds remaining. Loosen the first two reeds until they form an "M" shape. Take the end of the left reed and place it around behind the "M" shape and into the left side of the "M". Take the last reed and place it into the back of the middle hole in the "M" shape. Pull all the reeds tight and squeeze the rim to tighten it. Follow the same directions for the rest of the

rows beginning in a different place for each row. Always hold the reed as close to the gourd as possible. You will have to change the direction that you hold the reeds as you progress up and over the rim. Begin with the three reeds pointing to the middle of the gourd bowl, then straight up. As you go over the rim you will have to begin holding the reeds down towards the outside of the gourd bowl. This will make the woven reed curl up and over the rim of the gourd. Continue until the rim covers the place where the reeds were first inserted. Allow the reed to dry completely before trimming the ends. Cut the ends close enough so they pop under the rim, but be sure not to cut too closely.

Ending a row with the "M" formed by the spokes. *Photography by Derral Durrence.*

Random Woven Gourd Rim

Submitted by Angie Wagner, this is a woven rim that would be used directly on top of the gourd bowl. This is a fun and easy way to do some weaving on your gourd. Try different materials to weave the rim: reed, wire, paper core, or anything suitable.

"Random weave can be done in a very open and loose manner or the weaving is snug and can be continued until all spaces are filled and the weaving is very solid & tightly woven. Weave your random weave based on your personal weaving style and preferences."

Random Woven Gourd Rim.
Courtesy of Angie Wagner.

Frame: Drill holes around rim. Start anywhere around the rim with a short tail left on the inside of the gourd. Weave in and out of the holes in a random manner. Catch your starting end in a loop and pull loop tight against the inside of the gourd. Use an awl or fib to create space for your weaver if needed.

Drill holes around the gourd to weave the rim. *Courtesy of Angie Wagner.*

Start the frame by weaving the heavier materials in and out of the holes in a random order. *Courtesy of Angie Wagner.*

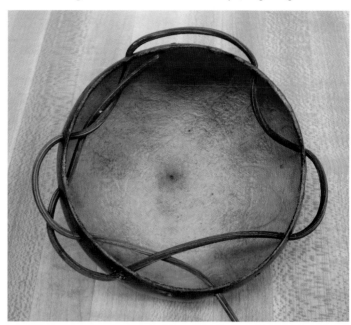

Keep weaving and overlapping. *Courtesy of Angie Wagner.*

End by hiding the ends inside the gourd. *Courtesy of Angie Wagner.*

Use an awl to open up spaces in the weaving. *Courtesy of Angie Wagner.*

Secondary Frame: Begin wrapping the secondary (medium weight) materials around the frame. Cut the end of the medium weight material on an angle. Hide or tuck the end into any spot that will hold the end securely. Take the material around the loops forming a secondary frame.

Use a medium weight material to start the secondary frame. *Courtesy of Angie Wagner.*

Randomly weave in and out of the first framework and end by tucking spokes inside and under other pieces. *Courtesy of Angie Wagner.*

Weavers: Switch to a lightweight weaver and weave over and under the loops. Weave in any direction. Always tuck the end of the weaver into a spot that is secure and hidden. Keep weaving to fill in the largest open spaces first. Depending on your preference, once the framework is in place, you can keep your weavers going in the same general direction or switch directions with each new weaver. If your weaver is flexible enough you can change directions sharply many times to get to the remaining open spaces. Keep weaving until you are happy with the appearance of your gourd rim.

Using different colors of weavers will display the random weave. *Courtesy of Angie Wagner.*

The last step is to weave over and through the frames with a lightweight material. *Courtesy of Angie Wagner.*

HAPPY WEAVING!

51

Chapter Six

Adding Pizzazz

Now that you are finished weaving the basket on your gourd, you are ready to add some fun things to embellish and enhance it. Try a dream catcher, tapestry weave, a pod or shell, some special weaving on the gourd itself, or maybe a crazy border. You can carve the gourd and inlay a piece of dichroic glass, or even glue on rocks and shells. Use your imagination and add some pizzazz!

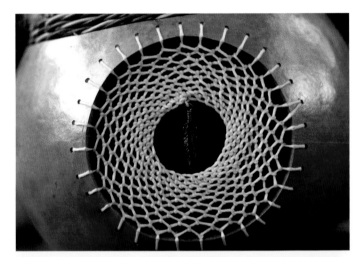

Dream catchers add pizzazz to the gourd. Here Maxine Riley used white thread and added a metal feather in the center.
Photography by Dorothy Kozlowski.

Adding pods can help enhance the gourd weaving.
Photography by Kelly Hazel.

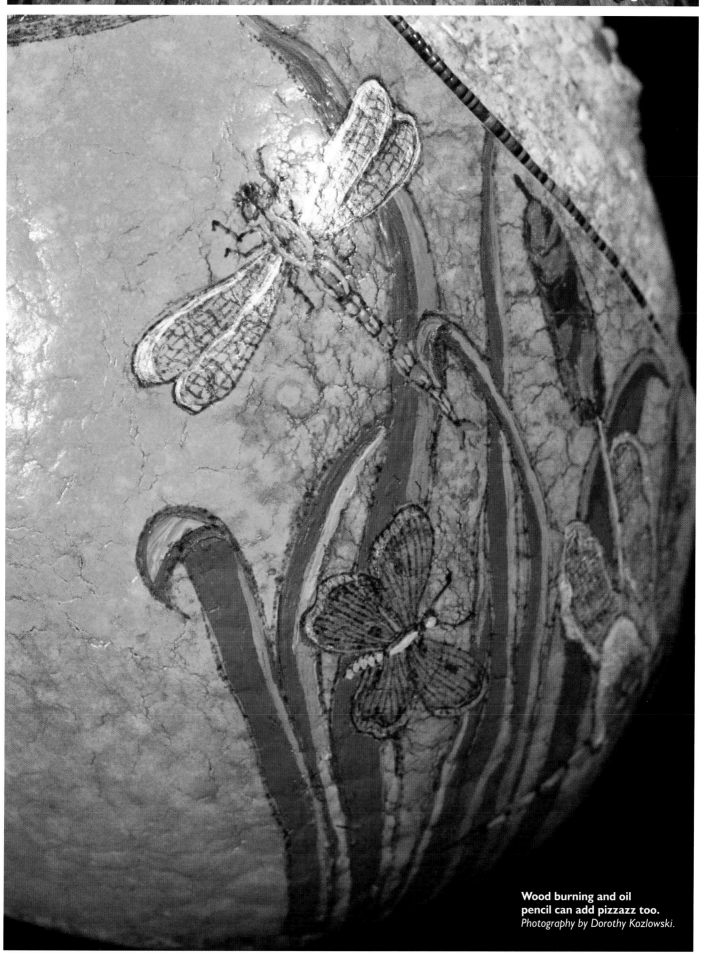

Wood burning and oil pencil can add pizzazz too.
Photography by Dorothy Kozlowski.

Dreamcatchers

I love dreamcatchers. It is a natural element to add on the front of my gourd weavings. A dreamcatcher is actually knotless netting. This is a technique that many gourd artist use to cover gourds. I taught elementary art for thirty-eight years. When my fourth graders studied Native American cultures, I supplemented the classroom teacher's curriculum by teaching them some Native American style arts and crafts. We made dreamcatchers on vines twisted to make a circle. I realized that I could cut a hole in the gourd, drill holes around the hole, and weave a dreamcatcher using waxed linen thread. One problem I had was that I thought you had to use only one long thread to weave the entire dreamcatcher. This was all right with a small gourd, but I used extremely large gourds. My faithful husband would sit in a chair in front of me and help me use an extremely long piece of waxed linen thread. Now if you have worked with waxed linen thread you know that it knots very easily. What a mess! It sounds crazy, but I did win my first major award with this gourd. It was a "Best of Show" award at the Upstate Visual Arts, "Art in the Park." Since then I wised up. I started using different colors of thread and devised a way to attach new pieces of thread. Below I have my pattern for making a dream catcher. Directions are given for a right-handed person. If you are left- handed, reverse the directions.

Cut a hole in the front of the dreamcatcher. The size depends on the size of the gourd and the size dreamcatcher you want to have. Drill holes around the hole you cut — 1/4" from the edge of the hole and 3/8" apart. The hole needs to be big enough for the needle and thread to go through. Choose two to three coordinating colors of waxed linen thread (if you want to change colors). Cut off about a two to three foot piece (enough to get around the hole at least one time and start on the second row).

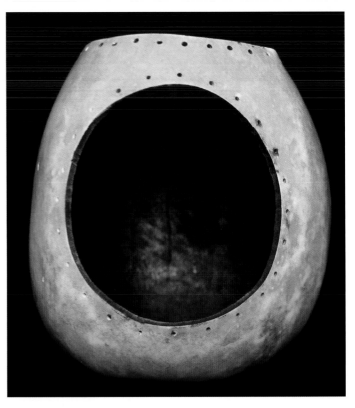

Prepare the gourd for the dreamcatcher by drilling holes around the hole. *Photography by Kelly Hazel.*

To begin, you will bring the end of the thread through the front to the back. Bring the two pieces of thread to the edge of the gourd opening and tie a knot. Pull the knot to the inside of the gourd. Another way to begin is to bring the tread from the front of the gourd through the hole and to the inside of the gourd. Tie a bead that is larger than the hole to the end of the thread inside the gourd. Use whatever is comfortable for you.

I used waxed linen thread or sinew for weaving the dreamcatcher. *Photograph by Kelly Hazel.*

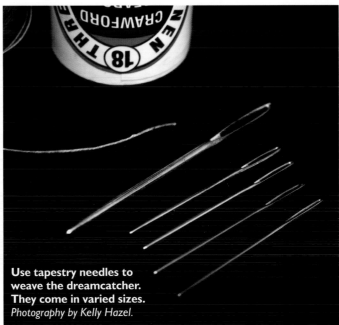

Use tapestry needles to weave the dreamcatcher. They come in varied sizes. *Photography by Kelly Hazel.*

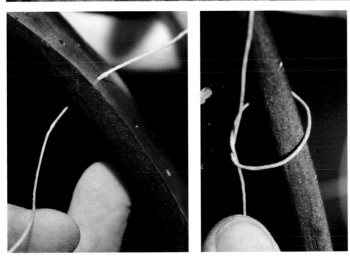

Pull thread through the hole. Tie on the waxed linen thread.
Photography by Kelly Hazel.

Go to the next hole. Go from the outside of the gourd to the inside. Come out through the loop in the thread. Continue doing this all the way around the gourd.

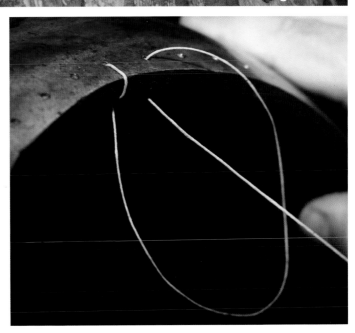

Pull the thread through the loop. *Photography by Kelly Hazel.*

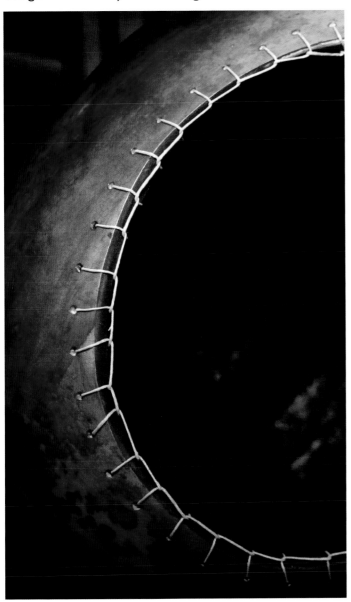

Tighten against the gourd. *Photography by Kelly Hazel.*

Do this all the way around the gourd. *Photography by Kelly Hazel.*

When you get back to the beginning, go in the first hole where you started. When you come back out, put the needle under the slanted thread made by the very first stitch and come through the loop of thread. When you start the second row you will not go through the holes. Bring the needle around the top of the thread and back through the loop. Make sure you see the cursive "e". Pull snug every time you come through the loop. Continue around the second row. It will form triangles. The third row and all consecutive rows will be done the same

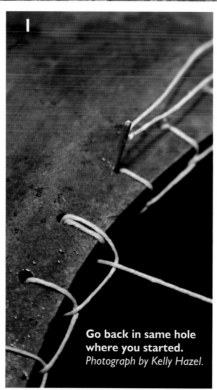

Go back in same hole where you started. *Photograph by Kelly Hazel.*

On the second row, you go through the loops that are tight against the top of the gourd. **Try to stay in the center of each loop.** *Photography by Kelly Hazel.*

Go under the thread and back through the loop. *Photography by Kelly Hazel.*

Do this all the way around. You will see triangles forming. *Photography by Kelly Haze*

Instead of going back in the hole, on this and all other rows you will go in the loops formed on the last row. *Photography by Kelly Hazel.*

Make sure you see the cursive "e." *Photography by Kelly Hazel.*

way. When you run out of thread you will add another piece. If you want to change colors, this is where you do it. Take the end of the thread you have been using and hold it straight out. Tie one end of the new thread to the old piece. Push the knot down to the weaving. Then take the new thread and the other piece of the old thread and tie another knot. Remember to keep the knot close to the weaving. Slip a small bead on the new thread and push it all the way down to the weaving.

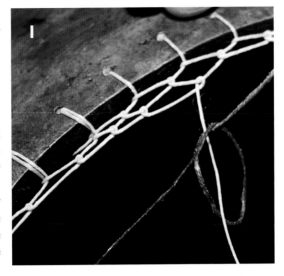

Adding a new thread. *Photography by Kelly Hazel.*

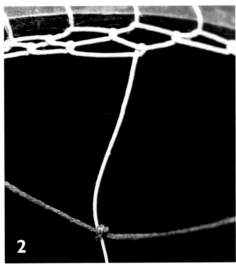

Tie new thread to old. *Photography by Kelly Hazel.*

Slide knot to the weaving and tie another knot. *Photography by Kelly Hazel.*

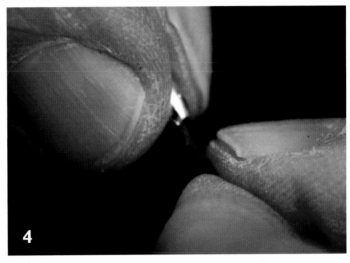

Slide on a bead. *Photography by Kelly Hazel.*

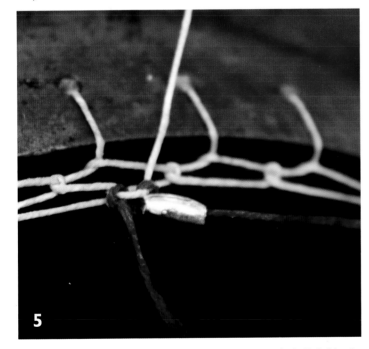

Keep bead close to knot and keep weaving. *Photography by Kelly Hazel.*

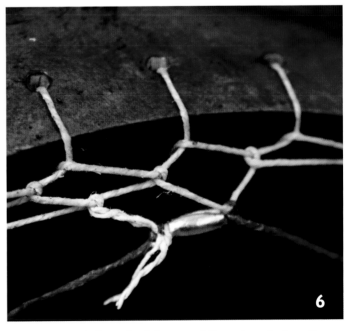

You can unravel the ends of the waxed linen thread where it was cut to add another design element. *Photography by Kelly Hazel.*

Continue weaving or knotting the dreamcatcher; you will change colors several times if you have a large gourd. When you have a nice size hole in the center, you will end by tying a knot. Unravel the ends of the string if you want to use that element as a decoration. You can also do this where you add beads or push knot to the back of the weaving. The last thing you can do to add pizzazz is to tie a charm or shell or special beads to the top of the dream catcher. This can go along with the theme of the dream catcher and woven basket.

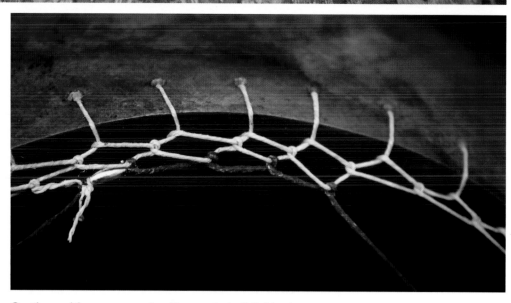

Continue with your new color. *Photography by Kelly Hazel.*

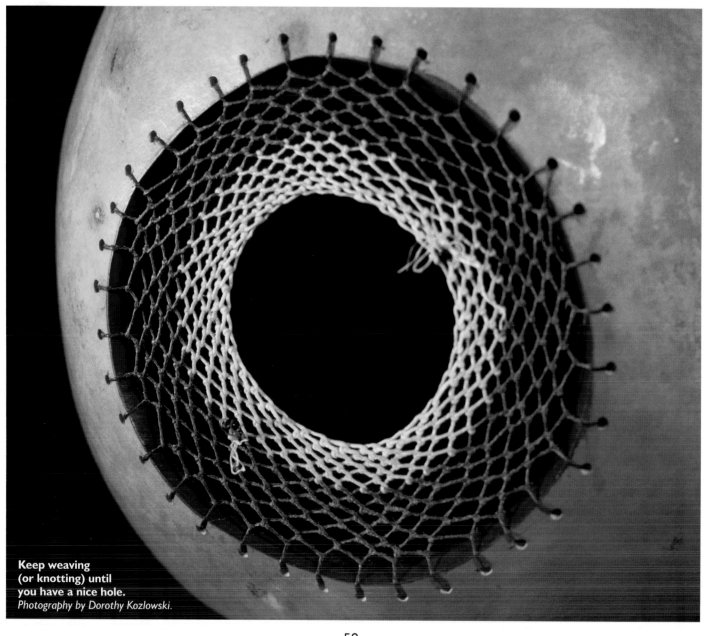

Keep weaving (or knotting) until you have a nice hole.
Photography by Dorothy Kozlowski.

**If you like you can hang a shell
or feather or charm in the hole.**
Photography by Dorothy Kozlowski.

Photography by Derral Durrence.

This picture is a variation on the dreamcatcher. It was woven by Laraine Short, a gourd artist and decorative painter from Florida. Laraine wove the dreamcatcher on the side of the gourd without cutting a hole. She drilled holes around the front of the gourd and started the dreamcatcher through the holes, inserting beads to cover the holes. As she wove, the dreamcatcher tightened against the gourd. Her rim is a beaded rim woven with wire around the top of the gourd.

Netted Beadwork with Gretchen Rim

Submitted by Cheryl Dargus, she said she got the idea for this dreamcatcher from a beading project in a book, *Creative Native American Beading* by Teresa F. Geary. Cheryl learned how to make a Huichol Lace Sun Catcher, also called open-lace netting, and adapted it for her gourd dreamcatcher. Most Hurichol lace patterns are worked from the center out, but the design for the netted beadwork dreamcatcher was worked from the outside to the center. The opening for the lace design was cut before the gourd was dyed and the rim added and the netted beadwork was completed last.

Materials

- Beading thread (such as Nymo®)
- Beading needle (size 10)
- Round eyelets (available at scrapbook supply stores)
- 3mm rounds
- 1/4" bugles
- 1/8" bugles
- Size 8 seed beads
- Size 11 seed beads
- Metal feather or your choice of hanging embellishment

Netted Beadwork with Gretchen Rim. *Courtesy of Cheryl Dargus*

Directions

This pattern is for a four-inch diameter opening. If you have a smaller opening you may want to use smaller beads in rows one through four. For this design it does not matter whether you have an odd or even number of holes. Using an awl or drill bit (I used a 1/8" drill bit), punch holes all around the rim of the hole, and approximately 1/4" from the edge of the hole and approximately 1/2" apart. Be sure that the eyelets will sit in the hole securely.

Row 1: Use a size eight bead to hold the knot at the end of the thread and bring the needle from the inside of the gourd to the outside. A size eight bead will anchor the beading from the inside. String one 3mm round, one 1/4" bugle, one 3mm round, one 1/4" bugle, and one 3mm round and bring the needle into the next hole to the inside of the gourd. It doesn't matter whether you bead to the left or the right as long as you remain consistent. Once the needle is on the inside of the gourd, place another size 8 bead on the needle as anchor and bring the needle out the same hole you just went in and through the 3mm round. This will give you one "V" shape between holes. Continue creating "V's". When you complete the final "V" pass the needle in through the first 3mm round to the inside, catching the anchor bead and bringing the thread out through the 3mm bead, through one bugle to the peak bead. This completes Row 1.

Row 2: String three 3 mm beads and pass the thread through the next peak bead. Continue adding three beads between each peak bead until you complete the circle. Run the needle through to the middle bead, completing Row 2.

Row 3: String one 1/8" bugle, one size 8 and one 1/8" bugle and bring the needle up through the middle bead of the three beads in row 2, creating a small "V" shape. Continue stringing one 1/8" bugle, one size 8 and one 1/8" bugle until you complete the circle. Run the needle through the beginning middle bead down through the bugle to the peak bead, completing Row 3.

Row 4: String three size 8 beads and pass the thread through the next peak bead. Continue adding three size 8 beads between each peak bead until you complete the circle. Run the needle through to the middle bead, completing Row 4.

Row 5 to center: Each following row will use 11 seed beads and will follow the same pattern reducing the number of beads in your "V" until you decide to finish it off. Begin with stringing four or five size 11 beads and bringing the needle up through the next middle bead in Row 4. Continue around and around reducing the number of beads in each round as necessary to fit the design. You can have several rows of the same amount of beads before reducing.

Last row: Once you have decided your design is complete, run your thread through all the beads on that row pulling it taut. Tie off by running the thread up through a few rows of beads and tie a knot. Add the hanging embellishment of your choice and your Hurichol Lace design is complete.

Embellishments

Adding embellishments really will add pizzazz to your gourd. Shells and pods are really fun. You can add them to the weaving or the philodendron sheath on the rim. There are many suppliers who sell embellishments, but you can also find your own natural ones. In the book *Nature's Embellishments* by Jo Campbell-Amsler, you can find many different ideas you could use on your gourds. Embellishments like willow beads, acorn buttons, and bark bows would give your gourd basket texture and interest. Found objects like junk jewelry, buttons, and feathers could also be used. I like to collect shells, so I add different kinds of shells to my gourds.

You can make the weaving look like a picture or landscape by adding some extras. In these photographs, I wove a fish using black ash and attached it to the water part of my weaving. I also used a large thick Chenille® stick to make a palm tree as part of the weaving. Experiment and have fun.

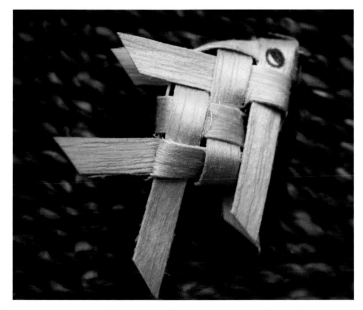

Palm tree was made with chenille sticks. *Photography by Kelly Hazel.*

Fish decoration woven with black ash. *Photography by Kelly Hazel.*

You can add pizzazz to your gourd by altering the gourd surface. You can carve out a space and inlay a cabochon. A cabochon is a gemstone that is flat on the bottom and rounded on the top. It can be any shape, round or free form. Dichroic glass cabochons are very intense and iridescent. The metals in the glass are fused in a kiln to create incredible results. They are beautiful embedded in a gourd.

Dichroic glass and wood burning.
Photography by Dorothy Kozlowski.

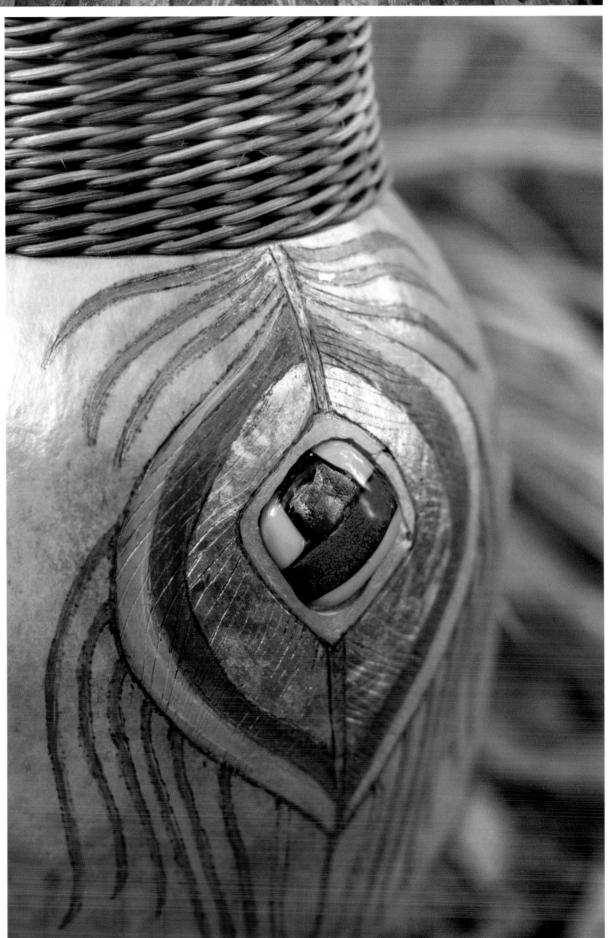

Dichroic glass adds a new dimension.
Photography by Dorothy Kozlowski.

Carving and adding elements are interesting decorations. *Photography by Dorothy Kozlowski.*

Carving your gourd and adding natural elements by gluing them on also enhance the appearance of the gourd. In this gourd called "By the Sea", I carved away some of the gourd and painted and wood burned elements of the design. To the carved area I glued small stones and shells and tiny starfish. This type of design can be added to a woven gourd as a complement to the landscape in the weaving. Be creative and add pizzazz to that gourd!

Other Fun Things with Weaving

There are so many ways you can weave on the gourd and then add extra elements to that gourd to adorn it. The photographs give you a few more suggestions. One way is to add a tapestry weave to the front of the gourd instead of the dream catcher. This one is called "Rhapsody" and it was woven by Marla Helton. Another way to enhance the gourd is to add an interesting rim. Jaynie Barnes left the weaving materials out to form an interesting element to the rim of the gourd basket. Debbie Wilson's weaving adds the pizzazz to her gourds. She weaves with varied materials such as sisal and actually weaves on all sides of the gourd. Jill Choate adds an antler to her baskets, so you could add one to your gourd weaving, and Susan Byra adds found objects. So you see there are so many ways to make that gourd unique. Have a great time coming up with some new ideas.

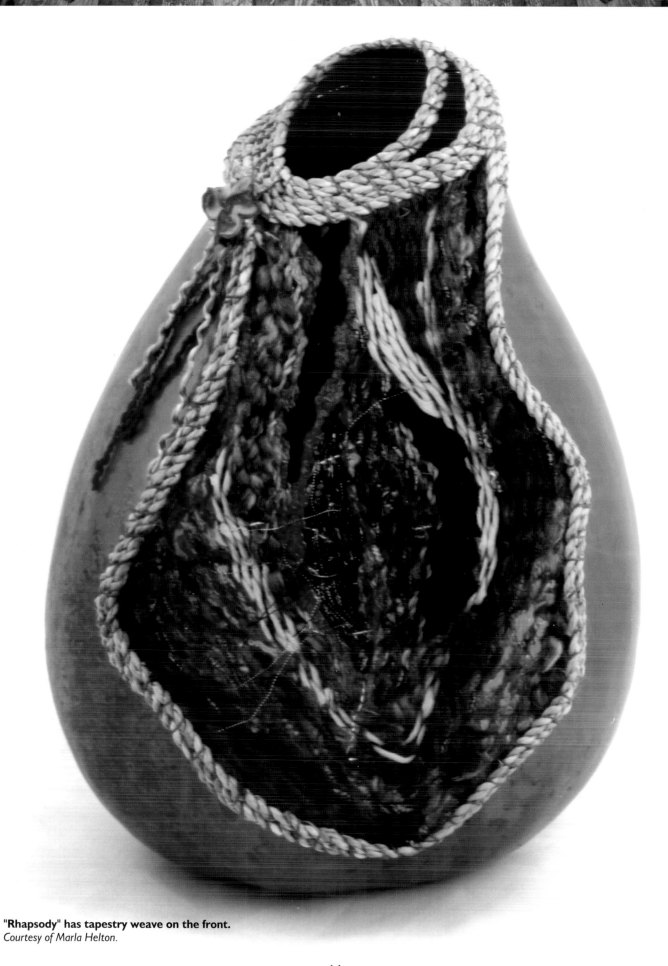

"Rhapsody" has tapestry weave on the front.
Courtesy of Marla Helton.

Interesting rim treatments. *Courtesy of Jaynie Barnes.*

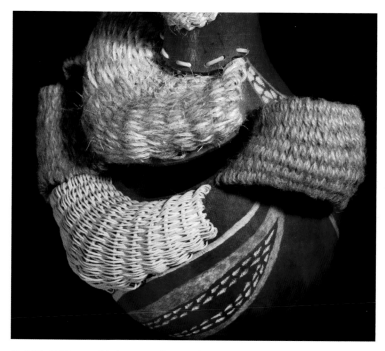

Debbie Wilson adds interest by carving and weaving on the body of the gourd. *Photography by Dorothy Kozlowski.*

Items such as buttons, jewelry, and ribbon can be added as decorations. *Courtesy of Susan T. Byra.*

Adding antlers can add pizzazz to baskets and gourds. *Courtesy of Jill Choate.*

Tips

The following are some tips to make your weaving easier.
They are in no particular order. Hope they help.

1. There is no dye that is colorfast. Make sure that your gourd baskets with color are not exposed to direct sunlight or fluorescent lighting for extended periods of time.

2. Don't soak your reed too long. It will become spongy. Three to four minutes is long enough unless you are using a very thick round reed.

3. If you overwork your reed it will become hairy. You can soak your weaving and while it is wet use a small torch to singe the hairs off. If this makes you nervous, just take sharp scissors and cut off the hairs.

4. Do not store your reed in plastic bags. It will mildew if stored in plastic. Use paper bags and label the bags as to the size and kind of reed.

5. If your reed is dry and brittle, add a capful of glycerin to your water to restore moisture.

6. When spraying your reed as you weave, turn the gourd upside down. Never keep water sitting inside your gourd.

7. Always keep your reed wet when weaving. Use a spray bottle to do this.

8. When your weaver runs out the easiest way to add a new one is by overlapping. End the old weaver behind a spoke and add the new weaver behind the same spoke and place it on top of the old weaver.

9. When weaving with a flat weaver such as cedar bark, you can add a new weaver by overlapping the old and new weaver for three or four spokes. Place the new weaver on top of the old one and weave together. If the weavers are too thick to weave with, use a knife and scarf down the old and new weaver for that distance.

10. A good bone awl is helpful when weaving. It can open up tight spots when you weave.

11. When you open a coil of reed, it seems to multiply. The best way to get weavers from the coil is to have someone hold one end of the coil. Pull it tight and pull a few strands out at a time. Carefully coil it back up when finished. Keep rubber bands or twist ties around each end.

12. Before drilling a hole in your gourd, use a sharp pointed awl and make a beginning spot for your drilling. If you do not do this, you can slip and drill a hole where it is not needed.

13. If dye bleeds on a piece of natural reed, use a Q-tip® and bleach to remove the stain.

14. Only natural and direct dyes can be stored. Store them in an airtight container.

Chapter Seven:

Gallery

I have many wonderful gourd friends who weave amazing gourd baskets. I have included some of their gourd weavings along with some of mine in the gallery. I know you will enjoy viewing them.

"Sunflower."
Photography by Dorothy Kozlowski.

"Undulating Tapestry."
Photography by Dorothy Kozlowski.

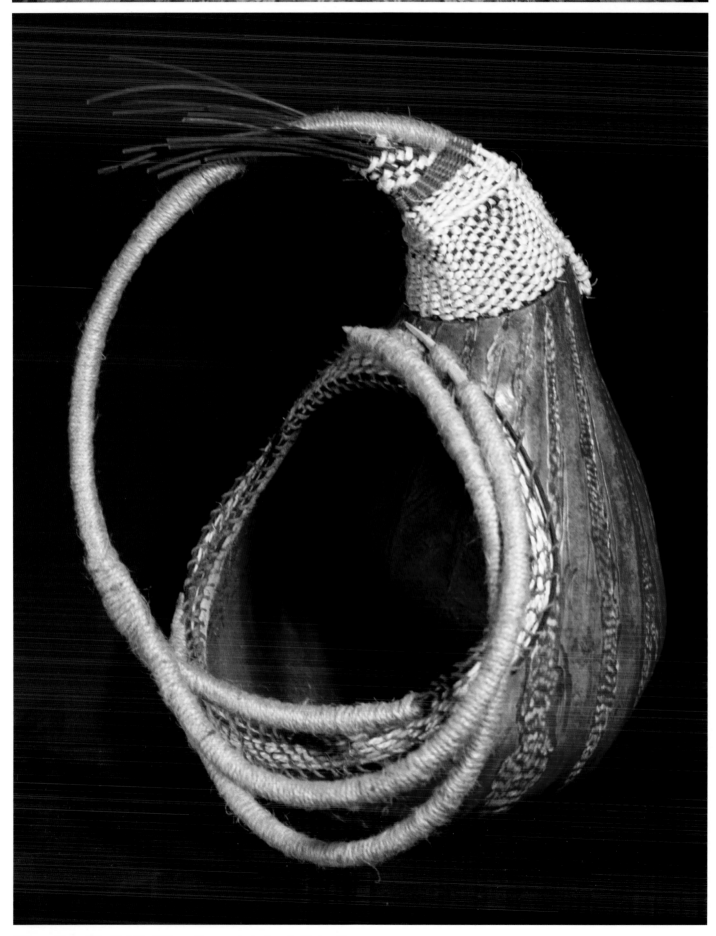

"Woven Gourd" by Debbie Wilson. *Photography by Dorothy Kozlowski.*

"Shells." *Photography by Kelly Hazel.*

"Undulating Gourd" by Karen Hafer. *Photography by Dorothy Kozlowski.*

"Contemporary Flower" made by the author.
Photography by Dorothy Kozlowski.

Undulating gourd with dreamcatcher by Maxine Riley.
Photography by Dorothy Kozlowski.

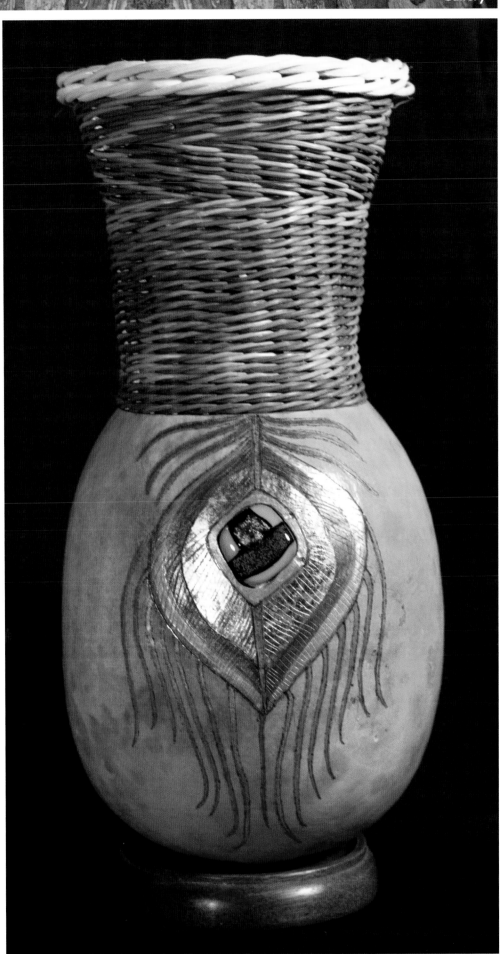

"Royal Feather" made by the author.
Photography by Dorothy Kozlowski.

**Woven vessel by
Debbie Wilson.**
*Photography by
Dorothy Kozlowski.*

Woven gourd by Debbie Wilson.
Photograpy by Dorothy Kozlowski.

"Kokopeli" by Vicki Plienis.
Photography by Rick Zimmerman.

"Allemande" was woven with waxed linen thread. *Courtesy of Flo Hoppe.*

"Gavotte." This gourd basket has a triple twine technique with spiral zigzags and darts. *Courtesy of Flo Hoppe.*

"Passacaglia."
Courtesy of Flo Hoppe.

"Minuet."
Courtesy of Flo Hoppe.

"Athena." *Courtesy of Flo Hoppe.*

"Polonaise."
Courtesy of Flo Hoppe.

"Spokes Galore"
by Marla Helton.
Scanned by Kelly Hazel.

"Bird's Welcome"
by Marla Helton.
Scanned by Kelly Hazel.

"Ti-Twinned Gourd"
by Marla Helton.
Scanned by Kelly Hazel.

Woven gourd. *Courtesy of Judy Ziegler.*

"Mizuhiki Metamorphis" by Marla Helton.
Scanned by Kelly Hazel.

"Tapestry Uprising" by Marla Helton.
Scanned by Kelly Hazel.

"Natural Harmony."
Courtesy of Marla Helton.

"Midnight Rising" — **twill weave
with waxed linen thread.**
Courtesy of Marla Helton.

Twined Gourd by Betsey Sloan.
Photography by Kelly Hazel.

"Blue and Copper Twill Weave." *Courtesy of Marla Helton.*

"Turquoise Arrows." *Courtesy of Patty Sorensen.*

"Double Philodendron." *Courtesy of Patty Sorensen.*

"Ebony." *Courtesy of Patty Sorensen.*

"Fall Colors."
Courtesy of Patty Sorensen.

"Tenerife." *Courtesy of Patty Sorensen.*

"Uncaged."
Courtesy of Patty Sorensen.

"Cherokee Wheels." *Courtesy of Patty Sorensen.*

"Variegated Gold and Red Metal Leafing." *Courtesy of Patty Sorensen.*

This gourd was woven with seagrass and filled with feathers and leaves. *Courtesy of Jaynie Barnes.*

99

"Spider" has a
dream catcher
that is not exactly
round. Made and
photographed by
the author.

"**By the Sea**" **is a very large thick gourd with a tapestry weave on top.**
Photography by Kelly Hazel.

This extremely large gourd won best of show at the Art in the Park show. This was the first major award won by the author. It was titled "Landscape by the Sea."

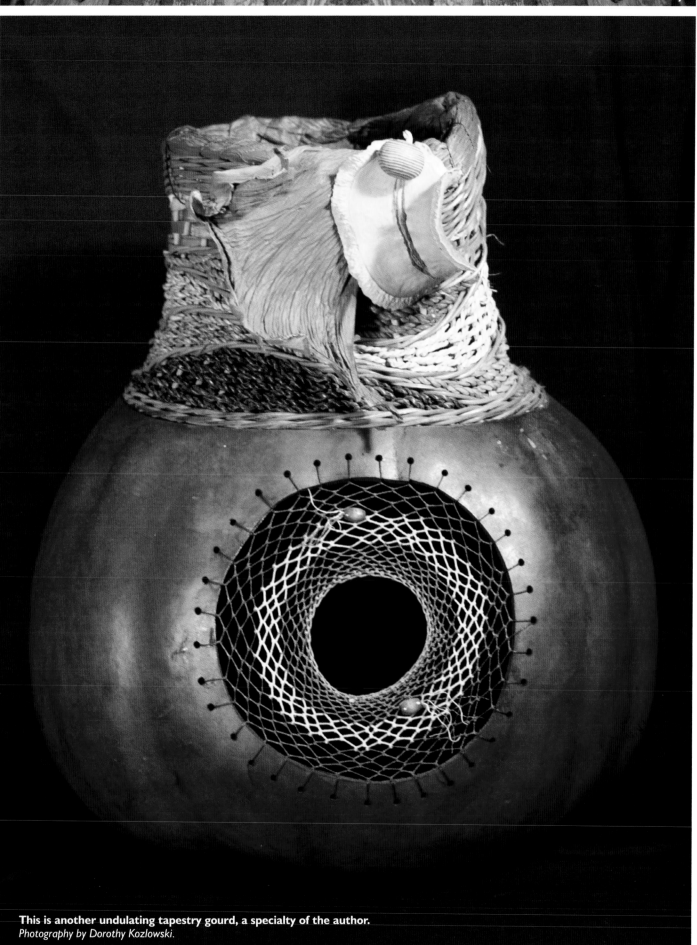

This is another undulating tapestry gourd, a specialty of the author.
Photography by Dorothy Kozlowski.

Jaynie Barnes, Earth Spirit Designs
www.earthspiritdesigns.com

Jaynie has been growing and crafting gourds since 2000 and has been teaching for six years. She has taught Gourd Art classes and workshops to students and staff at Smith College in Northampton, Massachusetts. Currently, Jaynie teaches classes and workshops for adults and youth at Hill Institute for Arts & Crafts. Her work has been exhibited at the Smith College Art Museum. Although, initially self-taught, she has studied with nationally renowned artists. Her techniques include carving, pyrography, beading, dyes, inks, oil pencils, rim ornamentation, macramé, crochet and basketry.

Jaynie attributes her passion for gardening to her grandmother, whom she also gives partial credit to for her love of Gourd Art, since it came out of the joy of growing her own gourds. She attributes her passion for the traditional arts, to her mother who was an avid sewer. Jaynie's work reflects her love of nature and her native ancestry (Cherokee). She finds it pleasurable and rewarding to begin the process of planting a seed, nurturing it into a gourd, then transforming the gourd into a piece of aesthetically, functional art. She loves foraging and incorporating natural materials and fibers into her gourd art.

Jaynie is a member of the American Gourd Society, the Pennsylvania Gourd Society, and a twenty-year member of the Northampton Community Gardens in Massachusetts. She sells her work at local shows and galleries and is currently working on a web site for her business. She holds a B.A. in Education, with 15 years experience facilitating groups, workshops and art groups with both adults and youth. She is passionate about bringing awareness to gourd culture and gourd art to local communities and to the New England area. Jaynie is known by her friends as "The Gourd Gal."

Susan T. Byra

A retired public library system director who got into gourd art about eight years ago, Susan is a multi-craft person (knit, crochet, cross-stitch, beading, and weaving are just a few of her talents). She had always wanted to learn pine needle

basketry, and as luck would have it, she met someone who was teaching a class locally and using that class as an introduction to gourding. Starting out with pine needle rim treatments, Susan has expanded her gourd repertoire to include pyrography, carving, and anything else she can think to try. An avid class taker at the Gourd Artists' gathering each year in Cherokee, she continues to search out and learn new techniques for her gourd work. Susan is founder and first president of the Mississippi Gourd Society, and an American Gourd Society Master judge.

Jill Choate, J. Choate Basketry
www.jchoatebasketry.com

Jill Choate is a nationally renowned fiber artist and instructor known for her ability to "talk to the antler" and weave a vessel around it. Her pioneering efforts incorporating antler into basketry have brought her to the forefront in this venue of contemporary vessel construction. Her efforts in

basketry are well known, as are her stories about life in the Alaskan bush. Now based in Missouri, Jill has lived in remote Alaska for twenty-five years with her family and sled dog team approximately 150 miles north of Anchorage. The Choate homestead was accessible by snow machine in winter and four-wheeler in summer and equipped with all the modern "bush" conveniences — like a hand pump and an outhouse. Living in the shadow of Denali with a salmon stream in the front yard and moose and bear for neighbors makes for great tales about life in the last frontier.

Cheryl Dargus

Cheryl lives in Arizona with her husband, and has been working on gourds since 2000 when she found a small listing in the newspaper about a patch meeting. She attended the meeting to find out what gourd crafting was and immediately got "hooked." Cheryl is a member of the American Gourd Society, the Arizona Gourd Society, and currently a member of three patches in Arizona (Old Pueblo in Tucson, Southwest Gourd Association in Phoenix, and Yavapai Gourd Patch in Prescott). She was newsletter editor for the Arizona Gourd Society for four years shortly after its inception.

Cheryl seems to be drawn more to embellishments on gourds instead of painting, carving, or wood burning. Cheryl won first place in the American Gourd Society's spring 2008 issue, Gourd Crafting contest. She won it with her basket woven "Samurai." The same piece of gourd art won first place at the Arizona Gourd Society competition at the Wuertz festival in 2008.

Charlotte Durrence

I painted my first gourd in 1993 and have been consumed by the desire to do many more. I still have that first gourd. It reminds me of all that I have learned over the years. I am a charter member of the Georgia Gourd Society and have held many offices in the organization. I served as first Vice-President of the American Gourd Society for one term.

Teaching gourd art classes have taken me all over the country and I have met so many wonderful people with the same interest. My husband, Derral, has been a great supporter in all things that I do. I love doing pine needle weaving and natural gourds.

Karen Hafer

Karen has always had an interest in arts, crafts, and designing with natural materials, having grown and arranged dried flowers for years. Upon retiring from teaching fifth grade for twenty-eight years, she studied floral design and became a certified floral designer. She now works part time in a floral shop. Six years ago, she took a community college course on gourd crafts. That opened up a whole new realm of design possibilities. Since then, Karen has been exploring gourd art, in which she enjoys the variety of expression possible. She has great interest in employing wood burning, carving, filigree, coloration, sprays, printing inks, rim treatments, and acrylic and watercolor techniques. She especially likes weaving. Since she first learned basket weaving, Karen spent many hours at the beach each summer on vacation constructing baskets. Now gourd basket weaving combines two of her favorite pastimes into one activity. Natural materials such as antlers, driftwood, feathers, natural fibers, seeds, and pods are incorporated into many of her projects. The rustic piedmont environment on her ten acres of land is a fertile source of inspiration from nature and animals. She is also drawn to southwestern and Native American influences.

Karen is a member of the American Gourd Society and Pennsylvania Gourd Society, as well as a local gourd group. She has won numerous blue ribbons for her gourds at county and state fairs. She lives in White Hall, Maryland with her husband, Henry, and her pet donkey, J.D.

Marla Helton, Serendipity Gourd Art
www.serendipitygourdart.com

Marla Helton became interested in mixed media in the late 1980s after taking a basket class. She began by combining weaving techniques with pottery pieces and soon moved on to weaving on gourds. She finds her inspiration in the shape and color of the gourd as well as interesting materials that she discovers in many of her travels.

Marla does art shows throughout the Midwest and teaches classes at retreats and conventions all over the country. She enjoys encouraging her students to follow their own creative instincts. For more information on Marla's work, visit her web site.

Flo Hoppe, Contemporary Basketry
www.flohoppe.com

Flo Hoppe is a full-time studio artist, teacher, and author. She began her career in 1971 teaching herself basket making from a small booklet published in 1924. Her emphasis is on wicker basketry and Japanese basketry. She lived in Japan from 1968-1971, and on a return trip to Japan in 1994 studied with two master basket makers. Her published books are entitled *Wicker Basketry* and *Contemporary Wicker Basketry*. She has also co-authored *Plaiting with Birch Bark* with Vladimir Yaris and Jim Widess. She teaches and exhibits worldwide, with teaching experience in England, Canada, Japan, Russia, and Australia. She lives in upstate New York with her husband of 42 years.

Terry and John Noxel

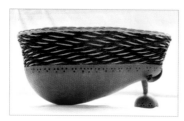

Terry Noxel has been an avid gourd artist since the late 1990s and is an active member and officer in both the Pennsylvania Gourd Society and the American Gourd Society. Terry has especially enjoyed combining other arts with gourds and has taken advantage of the versatility of gourds to expand her repertoire of crafts. Terry's husband, John, has been a self-taught weaver since 2005. John prefers small round reed and adapting his design on the fly. Combining gourds and weaving was a natural progression for both of them and have received many positive comments on their results. John resides full time in Windsor, New York caring for his family's small farm and building their retirement home. Meanwhile, Terry lives in Pennsylvania and works full time as an instructional designer and project manager in the training department for a major pharmaceutical company. They have two grown children and one grandchild who help Terry cleaning gourds and with her many craft endeavors.

Vicki Plienis, The Gourd Inn
Web: www.thegourdinn.com

Vicki Plienis is a self-taught artist who loves to work in many different mediums, gourds being her favorite. Her studio is on her resident property in an old renovated horse barn. It is filled with gourds of all shapes and sizes and many examples of her art. She gets her inspiration from her love of nature and traveling. On a trip to the Grand Canyon she discovered the kokopelli and fell in love with the many stories told them, and she decided to use it in a design. The gourd of Vicki's in this book has a kokopelli design wood burned on the front, and is colored with many different inks and finished with paste wax for a soft glowing sheen. The top is triple-twinned with many different textures and fibers, and is embellished with a tulip poplar seedpod.

Vicki is very proud of her two children, a son and a daughter, resides in Louisville, Kentucky with her wonderful husband of thirty-four years and her beloved yellow lab.

Maxine Riley

Maxine is an active member of the Upper South Carolina BasketMaker's Guild and the Palmetto Gourd Patch. She has been taking classes in basket making for many years, and uses many different techniques. She exhibits her baskets every year in the Senior Art Show, and has won many blue ribbons. Maxine combines her love of weaving with gourds too.

Sandy Elbrecht Roback

Learning about and making baskets became serious in 1985 and my hands haven't stopped since. I discovered my creative outlet! I have been instructing in basketry for the past few years because I enjoy passing along whatever skills or knowledge I have acquired.

My baskets contain three major design elements: color, pattern, and form. I enjoy seeing the play of color against color, the dynamics of twill and the challenge of a curved form. I've also been enjoying the challenge of weaving with painted papers. It is important to me that my baskets remain functional even though they may appear decorative. Craftsmanship is also a priority as well as respect for my materials. Hopefully my baskets are pleasing visually as well as tactilely.

Cass Schorsch

A master creator and teacher of fiber and bark basket techniques, Cass discovered her craft twenty-five years ago at a convention and has been hooked ever since. Mostly self-taught in her craft, Cass focuses on multiple techniques in basket weaving. This focus is clear in her works, which expand one's view of what is possible in basketry. Cass looks to Japanese basket weaving, which is especially complex, for her inspiration, as well as to the natural world. Cass has decided to narrow it down to birch bark and a little bit of cedar. The eastern white cedar is harvested from the upper peninsula of Michigan near the Hessel/Cedarville area. All the birch bark is from Vermont as the trees in Michigan have the blight or birch borer disease. Cass's work has been exhibited throughout the United States with a solo exhibit at the Boston Arts and Crafts society. Her work has also been published in numerous publications including 500 Baskets and Weaving History.

Laraine E. Short, Laraine's Creative Corner
http://www.picturetrail.com/agourdpainter

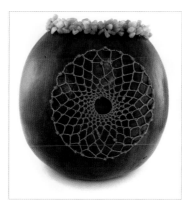

Laraine Short is a member of the National Society of Decorative Painters and president of the local chapter, Decorative Artists of Jacksonville. She is also president of the Northeast Florida Gourd Patch and the Florida Gourd society nominating committee.

Laraine teaches decorative painting classes at her studio, local and state chapters, art shows, art stores, local and state patches, and state and national conventions. She joined the American Gourd Society and the Florida Gourd Society in 2000. The same year she entered her gourds in competition and won her first blue ribbons for her gourd art. Laraine also received Best of Division in 2003 at the Florida Gourd show. She also received blue ribbons at the Alabama, Indiana, North Carolina, and Ohio Gourd shows.

Laraine likes painting her own designs and has over fifty pattern packets. In the last couple of years she has added inking, weaving, clay, and burning to her pattern packets. She also has designs in painting books by quick and Easy Painting, Plaid, and design books by sterling Publishing, Quick and Easy Gourd Crafts, and Glorious Gourds Decorating. Laraine loves to paint and doesn't feel like her day is complete if she hasn't picked up a paintbrush. You might find her in her studio around two or three o'clock in the morning with a paintbrush in her hand.

Betsey Sloan, The Pod Lady
www.thepodlady.com

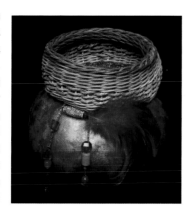

The Pod Lady is otherwise known as Betsey Sloan, a native of New England and a recent transplant to the south. Over the last fourteen years Betsey has taught at major art and craft schools. She has taught gourd art at gourd gatherings and private studios from Maine to Florida and as far west as New Mexico. She is certified in Art Silver and

Precious Metal Clay. She is the author of *InLace Resin Techniques*. She is active in her local gourd group and the South Carolina Gourd Society. Her website is called the Pod Lady.

Patty Sorensen, Artistic Gourds by Patty
www.artisticgourds.net

Born and raised in California, in 1975 Patty moved with her husband and two children to Richmond, Virginia, and then on to Houston, Texas in 1978. In 1995, with her husbands' retirement, they relocated to Montgomery, Texas.

Patty has always been involved with various forms of arts and crafts. For several years her passion was rubber-stamping. Many of her cards were published in national rubber-stamping magazines. After purchasing a gourd plant and growing some small gourds, she became intrigued with gourd art. When Patty attended the Lone Star Gourd Festival in October 2005, she received her first instructions in gourd art. She soon discovered it is work that she truly enjoys. Since that time she has attended gourd festivals in California, Arizona, and Texas and received additional training in various art forms. The techniques and elements that she uses on her gourds include pyrography, carving, painting, inlaid/inlace, pine needle coiling, Navajo coiling on Danish cord & paper rush. It also includes weaving with different types of reeds and other various natural grown plants. She has added basket weaving on gourds to her repertoire.

Patty has created several award winning art pieces, which are displayed and sold in galleries and private shows. She is a member of the American Gourd Society and the Texas Gourd Society. She has served as Secretary for the Tennessee gourd Society in 2007, 2008, and 2009. She has been part of the competition committee in 2007 and 2009. Patty belongs to the Southeast Gourd Patch and feels blessed to have found gourd art to showcase her artistic talents.

Angie Wagner, The County Seat, Inc.
1013 Old Philly Pike, Kempton, PA 19529
610-756-6124
http://www.countryseat.com/home.html

Angie Wagner was raised in a very rural section of Berks County, and she continues to live as close to nature as possible. Inspired by the patterns and colors she sees everyday, she works to create symmetry and

contemporary forms from chaotic natural materials. She grows and harvests many of the accents used in her work, which led to the name Woven Branch Designs. She specializes in round reed work and gourd art, but is always exploring new materials and techniques.

Debbie Wilson, Artbasgo

Gourd artist Debbie Wilson lives in the beautiful foothills of the Blue Ridge Mountains. She has taught art for over twenty years, and during that time has found herself a niche in gourd art. By weaving, carving, burning and embellishing, she transforms gourds into extravagant works of art. Debbie is a member of: Upstate Visual Arts, Trillium Arts, SC Gourd Society, American Gourd Society, Palmetto Gourd Group,

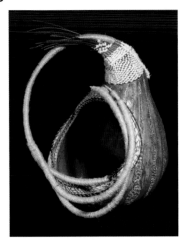

Metropolitan Arts Council and Chesnee Artisan Center.

Judy Zeigler

Since she was a child, working with her hands and creating things has always interested Judy Zeigler. A native of Sarasota, Florida, she attended Ringling School of Art and has a B.A. degree in art education from the University of South Florida. She began painting on gourds several years ago.

After attending the Second Annual Gourd Gathering in Cherokee, North Carolina, she was hooked. Gourds offer a limitless canvas to express ones artistic creativity. Judy currently does pyrography, painting, and basketry on her gourds. Judy's specialty is coiling with waxed linen thread to create sculptural pieces. She resides in Murphy, North Carolina, where she teaches gourd classes in her home and at the local gourd patch. Judy is a member of the American Gourd Society and Georgia Gourd Society.

Twill Woven Basket by Sandy Roback. *Photography by Dorothy Kozlowski.*

Suppliers

There are many wonderful basket and gourd suppliers. If you need a specific material, check with Susi Nuss. She has a site called BasketMakers (www.basketmakers.com) and on it you will find sources for your baskets and gourds. You will also find contact information for basket and gourd organizations. The following is a list of the suppliers I use for most of my gourd and basket supplies.

Bonnie Gibson's Arizona Gourds
Web: www.arizonagourds.com

Ghost Creek Gourds
Dickie and Linda Martin
2108 Ghost Creek Rd.,
Laurens, SC 29360
864-682-5251
www.ghostcreekgourds.com

H. H. Perkins Co.
www.hhperkins.com
(source for Nantucket leveler)

Lena Braswell's Gourd Farm
Rt. 1, Box 73,
Wrens, GA 30833
706-547-6784

Onno Besier
912-772-3911
(source for gourd cleaning tools)

Primitive Originals
344 Creekside Drive,
Leesburg, GA 31763
229-420-9982
www.primitiveoriginals.com

Royalwood, Ltd.
517 Woodville Rd.,
Mansfield, Ohio 44907
419-526-1630 or
(toll free) 800-526-1630
www.royalwoodltd.com

Suzanne Moore's N.C. Basket Works
130 Main Street,
PO Box 744,
Vass, NC 28394
1-800-338-4972
www.ncbasketworks.com

The Basketry Studio
281 Mantle Road,
Sequim, Washington 98382
360-683-0050
www.thebasketrystudio.com/supplies/
kathey@thebasketrystudio.com
(good source for cedar bark)

The Caning Shop
926 Gilman Street,
Berkeley, CA 94710
1-800-544-3373
www.caning.com

Turtle Feathers
PO Box 1307,
Bryson City, North Carolina 28713
828-488-8586
www.turtlefeathers.net

Welburn Gourd Farm
40635-D De Luz Rd.,
Fallbrook, CA 92028
1-877-420-2613
www.welburngourdfarm.com

Wuertz Gourd Farm
2487 E. Highway 287,
Casa Grande, AZ, 85194
1-520-723-4432
www.wuertzfarm.com/index.html

Glossary

Arrow: Two rows of triple twine weaving where the first row is regular triple twine and the second row is reverse triple twine.

Awl: A pointed tool like an ice pick used to make an opening in the weaving.

Border: The top edge of the basket that keeps the basket together. It is also called the rim.

Cane: The outer peel of the rattan plant.

Cedar: Type of conifer in the cypress family. The inner bark of the red and yellow cedar tree is used for weaving.

Coil: A reed coil wound up in a circle.

Continuous weave: Weaving with an odd number of spokes that does not stop at the end of each row but weaves continuously around the basket.

Cordage: A term used for any type of rope or string made by twisting fibers together.

Dichroic glass: Glass that contains multiple layers of different metals (silver, gold) metal oxides, and silica fused together in a kiln, making each one unique. This beautiful glass is used widely by artists and craftsman.

Embellishment: Decorating your basket or gourd with natural and man-made elements.

Gourds: Cucurbits, members of the cucurbitaceous family, and this fruit grows on vines.

Hairs: Splinters and feathering of the reed that can be eliminated by cutting or singing.

Hard-shell gourds: Member of the Lagenaria. It can be used for ornamentation, crafting, vessels, and general interest.

Jacaranda pod: The fruit from the sub-tropical tree native to South America that has been widely planted elsewhere because of its beautiful and long-lasting blue flowers. The pods are used as embellishments.

Japanese weave: Weaving taken over two spokes and under one.

Nantucket: Sturdy functional baskets that originated more than 150 years ago by the whaling crew manning the lightships off the coast of Nantucket Island, Massachusetts. The baskets are usually made with cane over wooden molds.

Overlap: The process of laying one weaver behind or on top of another weaver and weaving both as one until the old one runs out.

Philodendron: A large semi-woody shrub with enormous glossy leaves. The sheath is used for embellishment for gourds and baskets.

Plain weave: It is also called randing or simple weave. Weave is taken over one spoke and under one spoke.

Pyrography: The craft of decorating wood, leather, or gourds with heated tools.

Randing: Plain weave usually using round weave. Weave is taken over one spoke and under one spoke.

Rattan: A vine like palm usually found in tropical areas of Asia.

Reed: Flexible strands cut from the core of rattan and used for weaving.

River cane: Plant that grows by the river and needs much moisture. The Cherokee used it to weave twill woven baskets.

Row: This is when the weaver goes completely around the basket.

Sisal: An agave (succulent plant) that has stiff fibers use make twine and rope.

Spiral: A design formed with twills or waling, using a continuous weave.

Spokes: Material that forms the rigid frame for weaving a basket.

Step up: A weaving technique made at the end of a row or area of triple twine or waling. It steps the weaving back to its original beginning.

Sweet grass: Sweet smelling grass native to the southeastern United States, it is used to weave baskets.

Taper: Cutting a flat weaver for about two inches at an angle making a gradual slope ending in a point.

Tenerife: Decorative embroidery technique that is woven in a lace like pattern.

Triple twine: Three rod waling where you are using three pieces of reed to twine.

Twill: A weaving technique going over and under different number of spokes and the design steps up each row.

Twine: A weaving technique, also called pairing, that uses two weavers, which twist around the spokes.

Weaver: A flexible round or flat material that is used for weaving.

Wale: Pattern where the left weaver in a set (three, four...) goes over two spokes and behind one.

Bibliography

Campbell-Amsler, Jo. *Nature's Embellishments*. Monticello, Iowa: Willow Ridge Press, 1993.

Daughtery, Robin T. *Splint Woven Basketry*. Loveland, Colorado: Interweave Press, 1986.

Dellos, Maria. *New Gourd Art with Ink Dyes*. Fort Worth, Texas: Design Originals, 2007.

Devine, Catherine. *Coiled Designs for Gourd Art*. Atglen, Pennsylvania: Schiffer Publishing Ltd., 2008.

Geary, Theresa F. *Creative Native American Beading*. New York, New York: Lark Books, 2009.

Gibson, Bonnie. *Gourds: Southwestern Gourd Techniques & Projects from Simple to Sophisticated*. New York, New York: Sterling Publishing Co., Inc., 2006.

Gillooly, Maryanne. *Natural Baskets*. Pownal, Vermont: Storey Communications, Inc., 1992.

Hoppe, Flo. *Wicker Basketry*. Loveland, Colorado: Interweave Press, 1989.

Jordan, Sandra and Wells, Carole. *A Bevy of Baskets*. Smithfield, North Carolina: Crafter's Press, 1989.

Lumpkin, Beryl Omega. *From Vines to Vessels: A Vine Gatherer's Handbook*. Johnson City, Tennessee: The Overmountain Press, 1987.

McNeill, Suzanne. *Dream Webs*. Forth Worth, Texas: Design Originals, 1994.

Shaw, Robert. *American Baskets*. New York, New York: Clarkson/Potter Publishers, 2000.

Siler, Lyn. *Handmade Baskets*. New York, New York: Sterling Publishing Co., Inc., 1992.

Siler, Lyn. *The Basket Book*. New York, New York: Sterling Publishing Co., Inc., 1988.

Sloan, Betsey. *InLace Techniques Resin Inlay for Gourds and Wood Crafts*. Atglen, Pennsylvania: Schiffer Publishing, Ltd., 2009.

Stewart, Hilary. *Cedar*. Vancouver, British Columbia: Douglas & McIntyre Ltd., 1984.

Sudduth, Billie Ruth. *Baskets: A Book for Makers and Collectors*. Madison, Wisconsin: Handbooks Press, 1999.

Summit, Ginger. *Gourds in Your Garden*. New York, New York: Sterling Publishing Co., Inc., 1998.

Widess, Jim. *Gourd Pyrography*. New York, New York: Sterling Publishing Co., Inc., 2002.